making the
most of the
millennium

resources, ideas
and information
for celebration
and mission

Contents

How to use this workbook   2

Key dates   3

Worth making a fuss about   4

First focus: Beginners start here   7

Let's pray   11

Past participants   16

Present tense: Assessing where we are   20

Future perfect?   26

Generation 2000: Youth on the move   31

Millennium action planner   32

Community pride   38

A weekend to remember: planning for 31 December 1999   47

Pentecost 2000   57

Resources   63

3, 21 10

HOW TO USE THIS WORKBOOK

Making the Most of the Millennium is a resource for local churches of all denominations and traditions. It is intended to help them prepare appropriate activities focusing on the end of 1999 and the beginning of the year 2000.

It contains three kinds of material, most of which occur in every chapter. These are:

- **Briefing** This offers thoughtful background ideas to inform your discussions about the church's response to some aspect of the Millennium or of Christian involvement. These could be used by church leaders in their preparation of talks, or copied and distributed to church council members or other appropriate leaders who are thinking about the issues.
- **Speciality** This is a detailed outline for a specific event. It may be used as it is presented, or adapted to suit local needs.
- **Pick'n'mix** A cluster of brief ideas, the details of which are not usually spelt out, to stimulate your imagination and to help you think practically about appropriate activities. Addresses and phone numbers to help you follow up these ideas are to be found in the Resources file on page 63.

As with all workbooks of this nature, the user will need to adapt the ideas to specific local opportunities. Permission is given by the publisher for users to photocopy pages (onto paper or acetate) for study in a single group or meeting.

But the most important thing, of course, is to do something about the Millennium. None of us will live to see another one. And with the world around us having a party for what is in essence a Christian anniversary, the only way the real meaning of the Millennium will get across is if the churches make it known. It is not too soon to start thinking about it; 1 January 2000 is already closer than when you began reading this, and your strategy will need time to mature and the details will work best if they are carefully prepared.

WHAT? WHERE? WHO? AND HOW?

Find out more from our resources file!

P A G E   6 3

➤ *INTO THE MILLENNIUM – KEY DATES*

1998 Suggested theme: *Year of Hope*

August	Lambeth Conference of World Anglican Bishops
19 August	500 days
29 November	Advent Sunday
December	World Council of Churches Assembly, Harare, Zimbabwe: 'Turn to God, Rejoice in Hope'

1999 Suggested theme: *Year of Charity*

17 February	Ash Wednesday
4 April	Easter Day
26 April	250 days
23 May	Pentecost Sunday
28 November	Advent Sunday
25 December	Christmas Day
31 December	Millennium Eve
20.00	Suggested church service time
23.58	Candles, silence and Millennium Affirmation

2000 Suggested theme: *Year of Jubilee*

1 January	New Year's Day
12.00	Nationwide peal of bells and time of prayer
2 January	First Sunday of 2000; major civic and state services
8 March	Ash Wednesday
23 April	Easter Day
10 June	Global March for Jesus
11 June	Pentecost Sunday
3 December	Advent Sunday

2001

1 January	The third Christian Millennium begins...

WORTH MAKING A FUSS ABOUT

➤ *WHY THE MILLENNIUM MATTERS*

*There is a lot of fuss in the media about the Millennium. Christians should be glad, because it is a Christian festival. But like Christmas, it is already secularized. **Gavin Reid**, Bishop of Maidstone and Deputy Moderator of the Churches Together in England working group on the Millennium, suggests why we should take it seriously.*

Briefing: Why we should bother

Government recognition [of the Christian nature of the Millennium] does not mean that there will be Government activity to communicate the Christian message. Such a task rightly remains with the churches.

The United Kingdom is almost certainly unique in the way it is marking the Millennium. No other country seems to be making Millennium celebrations a part of government policy, but that is what Britain is doing.

The reason why this is happening, however, does not stem from much profound cultural thought or historical sense. It all goes back to the Act of Parliament that set up our National Lottery. In that Act it was decided that twenty per cent of all Lottery profits should be used to promote suitable projects for the Millennium. A Millennium Commission was set up to supervise the distribution of such funds.

And yet, for all this world leadership in such matters, no thought seems to have been given to the actual meaning of the Millennium. I asked a member of the Millennium Commission in 1995 how much the Commission had taken on board the recognition that the Millennium was a Christian festival and had no other meaning apart from that. The reply I was given was, 'That's an interesting thought!'

Which brings me to the reason why the Millennium is so important. We live in a country that has lost its cultural and spiritual memory, and that is a very serious national malady. An individual who has lost his memory is considered to be sick. Unless you know the story of your own life you are a disorientated person.

A nation that has lost contact with the story of its own life is just as disorientated. It literally does not know how to be true to itself. The churches need to see the year 2000 as an opportunity to help a recovery process. We have got to 're-mind' Britain about the story that shaped our values, influenced our arts, informed our laws and gave us our religion.

A chance to educate

For two years a group of us, representing all the major denominations as well as the Evangelical Alliance, have been talking with the Government about this, and we have achieved some success. There is now a greater recognition of the essentially religious nature of the Millennium; that it is based on a Christian calendar which was established in this country by the Synod of Whitby in 664; and that the calendar is itself a living pointer to the importance, and indeed to the reign, of Jesus Christ. Every year is 'Anno Domini' – a year of our Lord.

Government recognition, however, does not mean that there will be Government activity to communicate the Christian message in the millennial year. Such a task rightly remains with the churches themselves.

In 1996, the Churches Together in England published a position paper on the Millennium, entitled *A Chance to Start Again*. In it there is something akin to a churches' 'Mission Statement' for the Millennium: 'The task of the churches in the Millennium is to forge a link in people's minds between the year 2000, the name of Jesus Christ, and the possibility of personal meaning and public hope.'

We cannot expect a national or local government to do that for us. It is our task.

It reminds me of that story in the Old Testament when the children of Israel finally entered their promised land. As they crossed the dry bed of the River Jordan, Joshua called together representatives of the twelve tribes and told them to pick up a large stone from the river bed.

Later, they made a cairn of those twelve stones at their first campsite within the promised land. It was to be a memorial and to provide an opportunity for teaching future generations the nation's God-centred story. 'In the future, when your children ask you, "What do those stones mean?" tell them...' (Joshua 4:6-7).

When the number 2000 comes up in the calendar of the Western world (to the confusion of thousands of computers!) one question will be asked implicitly and explicitly: Why is it 2000? Two thousand years from what? When our children and our neighbours ask those questions, we must 'tell them'. More than that, we need to do everything we can to stimulate those questions. The Millennium gives us the best opportunity we shall ever have to 'name the name' in our conversations.

> *The Millennium year is the final year of the Decade of Evangelism. It provides us with the greatest opportunity we shall ever have to show that Jesus saves.*

A chance to re-evangelize

Some will want to see this as an opportunity for evangelistic missions. In many cases that may be right. There is, however, another sort of evangelism that we must all take seriously and that is the evangelizing – or re-evangelizing – of our culture. That is why the churches at national level have been so concerned that the famous Greenwich Dome centrepiece of national celebration makes clear reference to Christ. That is why every local church either by itself, or preferably linked to others, should take every opportunity to reawaken the memory of the One born two thousand years ago.

We must, however, do more than simply 'name the name'. We must unpack the meaning of the name and we must do it in a clear and concerted way. This is why the Churches Together in

England Millennium Co-ordinating Group have put forward a logo with a family of messages. The logo simply says two key words that go to the heart of what Jesus can do and wants to do – *NEW START*.

Off the back of the logo there are three messages that we are hoping will break into widespread public awareness:

A New Start for the World's Poor
A New Start at Home
A New Start with God.

Those three messages hang together. The first draws on the Old Testament teaching about releasing people from debt and slavery whenever there is a jubilee year. The second applies the jubilee principle to what may be happening on our own doorstep. Both of these will strike an echo in many hearts outside of regular church membership. The third message brings us all back to the key factor. Before anything profound can happen there has to be *A New Start with God.*

The Millennium year is the final year of the Decade of Evangelism. It provides us with the greatest opportunity we shall ever have to show that Jesus saves.

FIRST FOCUS: BEGINNERS START HERE

➤ *MAKE A 'NEW START'*

As the run-up to the Millennium gathers pace, so will the flow of information. There is a danger that we shall be overloaded with brochures, schemes and plans long before we get to the end of 1999. Preparing for the Millennium could start to seem like a mystifying maze – or, worse, a minefield. A helpful 'way in' to Millennium planning is the New Start approach devised by the Millennium Office at Church House in London.

Briefing: The concept

New Start sums up the churches' approach to marking the Millennium. It provides a simple means to fulfil the aspiration that the year 2000 will be seen as a Christian anniversary and a major opportunity for personal, social and spiritual renewal. New Start is not a campaign driven from the centre: it is an umbrella concept under which a wide range of activities can take place. There are three key messages:

A New Start for the World's Poor
This focuses on positive action to reduce the inequality between rich and poor nations in the next Millennium. It draws on the Old Testament concept of 'Jubilee', when land was returned to its rightful owners and slaves set free.

The Jubilee 2000 Coalition, which already has strong support from the churches, has as its aim the one-off cancellation by the year 2000 of the backlog of unrepayable debt owed by the world's poorest countries under a fair and transparent process. For further information see page 29.

A New Start at Home
This focuses on positive action to address the widely-shared concerns about the way we live both locally and nationally. What sort of society do we want in the third Millennium? What kind of people should we become to achieve it?

A New Start at Home is a two-edged theme: it refers to issues to do with family values and life, as well as to concerns about social inequality and deprivation on home territory.

A New Start with God
This focuses on the wide range of mission, pastoral and evangelistic opportunities offered by the Millennium. This is the

NEW START is an umbrella concept under which a wide range of activities can take place.

churches' home territory and all over the country they will develop appropriate ways of naming the name of Jesus in what is, after all, *the* Christian anniversary year.

Two practical initiatives

During the Millennium period the churches will take two major initiatives:

- In December 1999, local churches will distribute a special commemorative candle to every household. The intention is that people take these with them on 'Millennium Eve' (Friday 31 December), and in a moment of quiet reflection, light them from one another in the dying moments of the century. The candles will carry the text of a special 'Millennium Affirmation' for the whole community to say together.

- The Feast of Pentecost (Whit Sunday, 11 June 2000) will be given over to major Christian celebrations, with events in which churches gather together, as did the first believers on the day of Pentecost, according to the Book of Acts (for further information, see page 57).

 # SOME STARTING POINTS

Pick'n'mix: Ideas for beginners

A Millennium ABC

This simple ABC offers another way of prioritizing as you make your plans:

- **Accept** Jesus Christ. Focus on helping people develop a relationship with Jesus Christ that will lead to a continual personal conversion – a change of heart.
- **Build** communities of faith, for it is within them that people are able to grow in faith, be strengthened through the word and sacraments, and be prepared for discipleship in the world.
- **Create** a more just and peaceful world. The mission of the church is directed outward. Let us work with renewed faith and energy in creating a culture of life within our world today. (*US Catholic Bishops' secretariat*)

Eight Millennium themes

The Churches Together in England paper, *A Chance to Start Again*, suggests a basic set of understandings and considerations from which churches need to work if maximum impact is to be made. Use them as building blocks in all your planning for the Millennium.

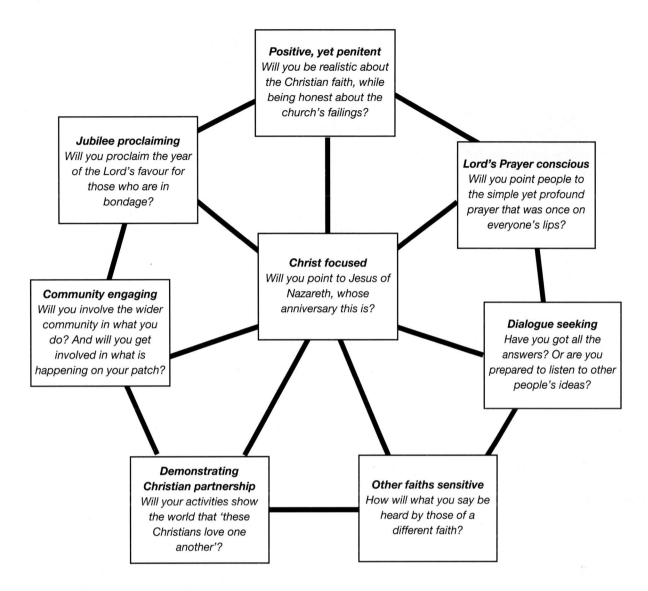

Positive, yet penitent
Will you be realistic about the Christian faith, while being honest about the church's failings?

Jubilee proclaiming
Will you proclaim the year of the Lord's favour for those who are in bondage?

Lord's Prayer conscious
Will you point people to the simple yet profound prayer that was once on everyone's lips?

Christ focused
Will you point to Jesus of Nazareth, whose anniversary this is?

Community engaging
Will you involve the wider community in what you do? And will you get involved in what is happening on your patch?

Dialogue seeking
Have you got all the answers? Or are you prepared to listen to other people's ideas?

Demonstrating Christian partnership
Will your activities show the world that 'these Christians love one another'?

Other faiths sensitive
How will what you say be heard by those of a different faith?

Pick'n'mix: Anno Domini

Anno Domini is an Evangelical Alliance initiative which aims to be a strategic servant and resource for churches committed to evangelism, social action and reconciliation in the build-up to the next Millennium.

It plans to help Christians be salt and light in their communities and aid churches to find imaginative ways of celebrating the greatest birthday of all time, and to ensure that the name of Jesus is central to all that is done. Anno Domini will be working with others in partnership towards 2000. It will achieve its aims through:

- a regular Millennium magazine
- worksheets on projects and ideas for celebrating our entry into the new Millennium
- regular news releases
- selected promotional opportunities
- a programme of managed public relations
- developing appropriate partnerships with Christian projects planned for 2000
- consultations with all involved in the Millennium celebrations.

Pick'n'mix: Badge up

The Millennium 'window' provides Christians with the opportunity to provoke and answer one simple but significant question – what made one man so special that the whole of history is dated from his birth? Y2000 is a resource to help Christians raise the question and to provide the answer by wearing an attractive Y-pin badge. The symbol Y is an ancient Christian symbol for the Trinity. A credit card-size leaflet provides the answer. On it the Y has been adapted in five ways, pointing to Jesus as fully God and fully human; Jesus on the cross, making forgiveness possible; the Trinity; a road that calls for a decision; and God's mercy and love. A range of Y badges and faith-sharing materials is already available – together with a video to show how to use the concept. A series of resources for churches to use the Y theme are in preparation.

Speciality: How to start planning

The churches in Greenwich are more Millennium-minded than most – they have the huge Millennium Dome and national exhibition on their doorstep. They have put together the following guidelines to assess what they do, and you may wish to test your own plans against them:

1. **Decide** who's going to start a proper planning process. Which church? Which other bodies? Who might we involve later on?
2. **Brainstorm** Discover, invent and adjust as many ideas as possible. You're looking for the right ones, so be prepared to discard plenty that aren't right.
3. **Test the ideas** by consulting: amongst yourselves, other groups, key individuals. And test them against the guidelines in the Churches Together in England's booklet, *A Chance to Start Again*.
4. **Who is it for?** Ask whether the activity is to be done by the whole community, by a few people on behalf of the rest or a bit of both. Is the balance right?
5. **Assess** which ideas are practical in the time available.
6. **Who does it?** An existing organization, or do you need a new one? If one church plans to go ahead alone, your activity will not be ecumenical, and you may need a new steering group to include others.
7. **Start now!** Make something happen. With the Millennium, postponement is not an option.
8. **Research** Who else is doing something similar? Don't be rivals, but co-operate, or even join forces. Learn from one another.
9. **Fund-raise** Do it after you have started, not before.
10. **Keep an eye on things** As you progress, test the activity, and check you've got the right structure.

And finally Ask this question: what long-term benefit does this idea offer
- our community
- the individuals involved
- the wider world?

WHAT? WHERE? WHO? AND HOW?

Find out more from our resources file!

PAGE 63

LET'S PRAY

➤ *THE PLACE OF PRAYER IN OUR CELEBRATIONS*

What's the link between prayer and the Millennium celebrations? Why pray at all for the Millennium? Surely it is just a moment in time and will all be forgotten by the next day? **Janice Price**, *Mission and Evangelism Secretary for the Church of England's Board of Mission, suggests some answers and says prayer should be central to all we do.*

Briefing: Focus on God

Birthdays with the big '0' make us ask questions about where we have come from and where we are going.

Why pray about the Millennium?

It is perhaps the greatest opportunity for mission and evangelism we shall ever know. We date our years from the birth of Jesus Christ, so we are marking 2000 years since his birth. When people ask, 'Why are we doing this?' the answer is because of Jesus Christ.

He is not just a figure in the dim and distant past but is alive and at work today. We need to pray that Christians will have the courage and boldness to talk about Jesus openly and freely at all times, and especially during the Millennium celebrations.

Isn't it just a passing moment?

Yes, it is just a moment in time. But moments in time are important. Think of the importance we attach to birthdays and anniversaries. The birthdays with the big '0' are the most significant. They make us look at our lives and ask questions about where we have come from and where we are going.

If this is true on a personal level, just imagine it on a global scale. Already many people are talking about saying sorry for past wrongs and are asking questions about the future of the planet.

Where should liturgy fit in?

The meaning of the word 'liturgy' is the work of the people. So liturgy is a communal form of prayer, remembrance and celebration. It is closely related to ritual. When significant things happen, people instinctively want to express what they feel, and they often do so through formal and informal liturgies.

For example, think of the death of Diana, Princess of Wales. People flocked to light a candle, lay flowers or sign a book of remembrance. These were informal liturgies of grief. In churches week by week we remember, celebrate and worship God, Father, Son and Holy Spirit.

So, at the Millennium, we will want to worship the God of time and express our hopes and fears for the future through

When significant things happen, people want to express what they feel, often through liturgies.

prayer and special services. For this reason an ecumenical group has been preparing worship resources for the Millennium. It plans to produce three worship resource packs to help churches to pray, worship and use this time to point people to Jesus Christ. These packs will include all-age worship resource materials as well as special prayers and some services.

The major themes which are going to be used in the Millennium services are: Reconciliation; Repentance; Waiting; Expectation; Renewal; and Light.

Pick'n'mix: Ideas for prayer events

Chalk it up

Create a graffiti board in your church beginning in 1999. Ask people to write, draw or scribble about their hopes and fears for the future and to write their prayer requests for the Millennium. Use these prayer requests in the intercessions in the main service or at prayer meetings. Take a different subject for prayer each week.

Let the children go!

Plan some young people's worship services, but as you do listen to those who will live most of their lives in the new Millennium. Gather a group of young people and help them to create a worship service looking forward to the new Millennium using the major themes we are all sharing.

Organize a prayer collection

Ask people of all ages to write a prayer for the Millennium. This will help them to express their thoughts and feelings about the Millennium and to turn them into prayers. Then collect the prayers together and produce a prayer book for the Millennium, especially for your church. You could offer a small prize for the prayers which most originally convey people's feelings and longings.

Light a prayer lamp

Special prayer lamps, made from traditional miners' lamps, are being suggested as one way of reminding everyone to pray that Jesus will be the light of the Millennium celebrations. The lamp, which is to be kept alight until midnight on 31 December 1999 (when the Millennium candles will be lit) is fuelled by paraffin and will burn for forty-eight hours with one filling.

Speciality: A service outline focusing on time

The suggested hymns and songs may be found in several books. The numbers given are for Mission Praise *(combined edition). The congregation is invited to say the words in* **bold**.

Theme: 'Jesus Christ – Lord of Time'; *or* 'How we use our time'.

Welcome

Leader: We meet in the name of the God of all time.
All: **He is here with us now.**

Hymn or song
All people that on earth do dwell (20)
At the name of Jesus (41)
Come let us worship Christ (96)

Confession
God of the ages,
Sustainer of the universe,
Look upon us with eyes of mercy
As we remember our errors and failings.
For the times
When we have not honoured your name,
When we have failed to be at peace with one another,
When we have abused your creation,
Forgive us, we pray,
Through your Son our Lord Jesus Christ. Amen.

Absolution
In the name of the God of Love,
In the name of the Prince of Peace,
In the name of the Spirit of Comfort,
May your sins be forgiven
And may you be restored to new life. **Amen.**

Statement of faith
Song: We believe in God the Father (720)

Bible Reading
Old Testament – Ecclesiastes 3:1-8 (A time for everything)
New Testament – Luke 10:30-37 (The Good Samaritan)

Suggested sermon outline
The reading from Ecclesiastes tells us that there is a time for
everything. There is time for all the experiences of life – to cry and
to laugh, to tear and to mend. The parable of the Good Samaritan
tells us about people who did not have time to stop and help a
sick and dying person. Only the Samaritan took time.

Celebrating the Millennium is about marking the passage of
time. It should cause us to evaluate how we use our time. Do we
have time for the unloved and unlovely, those in need as well as
those close to us? The actions we take in time also have an eternal
destiny.

The Lord of time himself said, 'I tell you the truth, whatever
you did not do for one of the least of these, you did not do for me.
Then they will go away to eternal punishment, but the righteous
to eternal life' (Matthew 25:45,46). How do we use our time? Who
is the Lord of our time?

Songs
Meekness and majesty (465)
Holy, holy, holy is the Lord (239)

Intercession

For all the forgotten and unwanted people
Help us to make time, Lord.

For those we love and cherish
Help us to make time, Lord.

For being with you
Help us to make time, Lord.

For telling others about you
Help us to make time, Lord.

For ourselves
Help us to make time, Lord.

Hymn or song
O God, our help in ages past (498)
Lord, the light of your love is shining (445)
Our God reigns (249)

Blessing

 # PRAYER RESOURCES

There is plenty of money being thrown at the year 2000. There are projects great and small. But silently, and almost unnoticed, there is a wave of prayer, too. These prayers may help you to join in.

Looking back
We stand with awe at the turning of history.
We marvel at two thousand years of grace.
We are ashamed of so much human sin and selfishness
which have marred God's beautiful creation.
We pray that the evil of the past may be wiped away
as we remember with thanksgiving God's saving act
two thousand years ago.

We pray that the name of Jesus Christ,
the lamb of God who takes away the sin of the world,
may be honoured in our celebrations
and continue to be a joy and inspiration to all people. Amen.
(The Rev Simon Baynes, St Mary, Winkfield, Berkshire)

Looking ahead
God of all ages, Lord of all time,
you are the Alpha and Omega,
the origin and goal of everything that lives:
yet you are ever close to those who call on you in faith.

We look with expectant joy
to the Jubilee of your Son's coming among us
two thousand years ago.
We thank you for the years of favour
with which you have blessed your people.

Teach us to share justly the good things
which come from your loving hand;
to bring peace and reconciliation
where strife and disorder reign;
to speak out as advocates for those who have no choice;
and to rejoice in a bond of prayer and praise
with our sisters and brothers throughout the world.

When Christ comes again in glory
may he find us alive and active in faith,
and so call us to that kingdom
where with you and the Holy Spirit,
he is God, to be praised, worshipped and glorified,
both now and for ages to come. Amen.

(CAFOD Millennium Prayer, Matthew James Publishing Ltd)

Looking around

God the Father, creator of justice and mercy:
God the Son, bringer of change and hope:
God the Holy Spirit, source of inspiration and help:
we ask your blessing on us, your pilgrim people of (*insert the
name of your community / neighbourhood / village / town / city*),
divided by traditions, yet united in longing to follow you.
Encourage us to face the Millennium in sorrow for our failings in
the past,
in hope of a change of heart
and for faith in a future built on your gospel of love.
Amen.

Generous God, you created this world for all to share:
Unclench our hands to let go of the greed which robs the poor;
Unclog our ears to hear the agony of all who cry for justice;
Unbind our hearts to recognize those who are oppressed by debt;
Open our lips to proclaim jubilee in our own time and place.
May our care be thorough, and our solidarity active;
May this community be a sign of hope:
For now is the favourable time. Amen.

(St Michael's Parish, West Derby, Liverpool)

**WHAT?
WHERE?
WHO?
AND HOW?**

Find out more from
our resources file!

PAGE 63

See also 'Community Prayer
Cells', *page 44*

➤ ## *LOOK BACK IN GRATITUDE, CELEBRATION – AND SENSITIVITY*

'Two thousand years of Christian civilization: let's hear it for the world faith that brought us architectural wonders, musical masterpieces, museums full of paintings, sculptures and manuscripts – not to mention loads of saints, missionaries and philanthropists. (But, please, soft pedal the fall-out of the occasional Crusade, witch-burning and "war of religion"...).'
Hopefully no one will try to hijack the Millennium as a vehicle for Christian triumphalism like that. It would be equally sad if we restricted ourselves to the acknowledgement of past sins. The coming celebrations offer a timely opportunity to look back and celebrate the positive aspects of a heritage which – by any estimation – is awe-inspiring in its depth and variety, as **Rory Keegan**, *on the staff of CPAS, explains.*

Briefing: Positive, yet penitent

Most of us are all too aware of past events that leave Western Christians with little cause for celebration, and plenty for repentance and restitution. You don't have to probe far beneath the surface of the 'heritage industry' to reveal basket-loads of historical dirty washing. An easily identifiable example is the violent injustice meted out to Jewish people in medieval England; another is the fact that slave-trade profits underlie the civic wealth of some of our great port cities.

It is right that we acknowledge past wrongs, seek reconciliation and commit ourselves to the pursuit of peace and justice. But it would be tragic to be so concerned with the negative aspects of our Christian heritage that we become blind to the vast contribution that the church and individual Christians have made to improve the lives of others locally, nationally and internationally. Similarly, it can't do anything but good to thank God 'for all the saints' (some officially recognized, most completely forgotten) who have faithfully and courageously 'passed on the torch' to us.

So how should we look back positively yet penitently? Much will depend on local circumstances: in some places research will reveal an embarrassment of riches, in others it may be necessary to take a more imaginative or creative approach. The following suggestions offer a variety of starting points.

Pick'n'mix: All Saints and All Souls

Commercial celebrations of Hallowe'en on 31 October have overshadowed traditional commemoration of All Saints Day (1 November) and All Souls Day (2 November). Both festivals provide ready-made opportunities for marking the lives and achievements of ordinary men and women. They coincide with traditional services and acts of remembrance for those who died in the twentieth century's military conflicts. Linking them to the 'Millennium mood' may provide a helpful way of quietly recognizing people who might otherwise be passed over in the noisier aspects of the celebrations.

A service of thanksgiving

Many churches already offer an annual service of remembrance and thanksgiving to people who have been bereaved in the preceding twelve months, or who wish to take the opportunity to thank God for the life of loved ones, regardless of how long ago they may have died. It may be appropriate in November 1999 to include in such a service a 'decade by decade' summary of the century. As people enter at the start of the service, give them the opportunity to take a single flower (or more, if they wish to commemorate more than one person). At an appropriate moment invite them to bring these to the front of the church where the single blooms could be combined into a memorial arrangement.

A celebration of saints

Research the history of your congregation, church building and community to reveal the 'hidden' stories of people whose contributions may otherwise be overlooked. Invite members of the congregation and community to recall significant people from each decade of the century. The 'mosaic of memories' that emerges could form the basis of a variety of activities:

● an exhibition
● a thanksgiving service
● a feature in the local press.

Pick'n'mix: Grave matters

Many churches have a ready-made historical archive in their churchyard. Gravestones and monuments provide a fascinating insight into the history of both church and community. Find out how many centuries are represented in your patch. Select a representative grave from each one and research the possible major 'life-shaping events' of its owner.

For example, a woman with the dates 1850-1940 would have experienced vast social, cultural and economic changes in a life-span that ranged from the Great Exhibition to the Battle of Britain. You may want to involve your local school or historical society in the project. Use the information gathered as resource material for a service of thanksgiving, for a special edition of the church magazine or for input into larger-scale community projects.

Pick'n'mix: Amazing saints

The church's official calendar of 'Festivals and Greater Holy Days' and 'Lesser Festivals and Commemorations' provides a rich and rarely explored resource of stories, inspiration and example. Why not select a 'saint of the week' for each Sunday in 1999? Give him or her a brief paragraph in the notice sheet – or take time in the prayers to thank God for that person's life and example.

What follows is a selection 'for starters'. You could also include saints who have particular local significance.

January
25 Paul, apostle
26 Timothy and Titus, companions of Paul
28 Thomas Aquinas, theologian

February
27 George Herbert, priest, pastor and poet

March
1   David, patron saint of Wales
17 Patrick, patron saint of Ireland
19 Joseph, husband of Mary
21 Thomas Cranmer, Archbishop of Canterbury, martyr

April
23 George, patron saint of England
25 Mark the Evangelist

May
1   Philip and James, apostles
8   Julian of Norwich, mystic
24 John and Charles Wesley, evangelists
26 Augustine, first Archbishop of Canterbury

June
9   Columba, Abbot of Iona
22 Alban, first British martyr
24 John the Baptist

July
3   Thomas, apostle
6   Thomas More, martyr
22 Mary Magdalene
25 James, apostle
29 William Wilberforce, social reformer

August
24 Bartholomew, apostle
     Augustine of Hippo, teacher of the faith
31 John Bunyan, author, prisoner of conscience

September
8   Mary, mother of Jesus
21 Matthew, apostle

October
4   Francis of Assisi
6   William Tyndale, Bible translator
15 Teresa of Avila, mystic
18 Luke the Evangelist

November
17 Hilda, Abbess of Whitby
30 Andrew, apostle and patron saint of Scotland

December
3   Francis Xavier, missionary
26 Stephen, the first martyr
29 Thomas Becket, Archbishop of Canterbury, martyr

(An expanded version of this list may be found in The Alternative Service Book 1980, pages 17-21.)

Alternatively, compile your own list of twentieth-century saints.

Speciality: Home group Bible study

Look back in wonder: Psalm 44

Key verse: It was your right hand, your arm, and the light of your face, for you loved them (Psalm 44:3).

Icebreaker (10 minutes)
Get each person to write down one event in the past which they now look back to as a highlight of their lives. Ask some (or all) briefly to say what it is and why it was significant.

Discuss (10 minutes)

Every culture (and generation) tends to look back to a 'golden age' which seems to have been 'better' than life today. To what extent is it really true? And why do we do it?

Read and reflect (5 minutes)

Psalm 44

Note: This psalm was written after Judah (the southern kingdom) suffered a major military defeat, but the precise event cannot be identified. The author is struggling with the fact that the defeat cannot easily be blamed on some obvious national guilt (verses 17-22).

Analyze and apply (30 minutes)

1. What sort of event is the psalmist recalling in verses 1-3 (e.g. Exodus 14; Joshua 5:13 – 6:27)? What was the secret of those successes? List some great events which Christians can look back on with wonder and gratitude. (Think about the church generally, as well as about personal examples.)

2. God's people are oppressed; progress has ceased (verses 9-16). Allowing for the fact that sin is not the simplistic cause (verses 17-18), why might the reversal have occurred? Think of reasons why churches and individuals go through periods of decline or spiritual staleness. List them, and discuss how they might be remedied or coped with.

3. The psalmist is determined to climb out of the present pit because he knows from past experience that things could be different. How does he go about it? (See verses 23-26 and compare with verses 4-8.) How could you apply this to your church's thinking about its Millennium activities?

Quote to note and discuss (10 minutes)

'A wheel is the sublime paradox. One part of it is always going forward and the other part is always going back... Every sane soul or state looks at once backwards and forwards; and even goes backwards to come on' (G.K. Chesterton). Make a list of the virtues and dangers of looking back to past events (e.g. avoid making the same mistake / expect the past to be repeated). How might these apply to your group or church today? What should be the relationship between the past and the future?

Prayer and praise (10 minutes)

Reflect quietly on what you have written down about past events and allow a sense of gratitude to form in you. Then use these things as topics for praise. Use what you know of God's character as the basis for prayer that he will work again powerfully (but in different ways) in the future.

PRESENT TENSE:
ASSESSING WHERE WE ARE

➤ *WANTED: A STORY TO LIVE BY*

*The world around us seems confused about beliefs and behaviour. Understanding contemporary society is the first step to addressing the gospel message accurately to it. **Derek Williams**, author and honorary curate of St Giles, Northampton, sketches the scene.*

Briefing: A state of confusion

Driving somewhere in the wilds of southern England, I caught a fleeting glimpse of a new supermarket. It had a high gabled roof with a central bell tower; it looked like a modern church. And across it was emblazoned: *Open on Sundays.*

'Shopping,' wrote journalist Victoria Mather after a trip to Harvey Nichols' new store in Leeds, 'has now graduated from a pastime to a way of life... We are validated by having entered the temple, made our offering by credit card and departed with our prayers answered in a sleek shopping bag, the name on which inspires recognition and envy. No wonder people spend more time in shops than in church on Sundays' (*Telegraph* magazine, 28 September 1996).

Many toys
As the traumatic and changeful twentieth century brings the turbulent and restless second Millennium to a close, the acquisitive society provides a footbridge into the future. Obsessed with gadgets and committed to the Cult of the New, we fill our household shrines with electronic totems of social virility.

By AD2000 some 150 TV channels will beam at Britain a mind-numbing mix of soaps, scoops, stunts, sport and sex. Smartboxes will link TVs to the Internet and bring cyber communities and on-line shopping within reach of the remote control.

No peace
But we are no happier. In 1997 Leeds University researchers found that a majority of people do not trust others. A Gallup Poll in 1996 suggested that seventy-five per cent of the population believe they have less peace of mind than in the past.

In the post-modern haze, old certainties have crumbled like a stale biscuit. God is dead; moral consensus has disappeared; and science has lost its confidence as the genie of the lamp. The icons of image are borne aloft by the high priests of spin who process a discreet step behind political, entertainment or sporting idols. We do not know who or what to believe, so end up believing anything.

As philosopher Roger Scruton puts it, 'a new post-modern society has emerged in which niceness stands higher than goodness in the scale of accepted ideals' (*Time*, 27 October 1997).

A story to live by

Somewhere, though, deep in the corporate psyche, a slumbering spiritual giant is stirring. A medley of folk religion, superstition, wishful thinking, vaguely-defined 'spirituality', half-remembered Christianity, a desire for guidelines but a fear of intolerance is being explored by everyone from media personalities to the people next door.

Caught in the cross fire is the church. The fabled decline in membership and attendance shows signs of slowing and, in some quarters, of being reversed. But the Christian light is split into many beams of differing colours by the prisms of denominational and theological distinctions, and the world is blinded and confused rather than enlightened and comforted.

The Millennium gives the church a unique opportunity to speak with one voice to a world more familiar with clerical vices than spiritual truths. It possesses what society seeks, which in the words of Reith Lecturer Marina Warner is 'a story to live by'.

➤ *HOW VISITOR-FRIENDLY IS YOUR CHURCH?*

*It would be a tragic irony if churches directed energy and enthusiasm into exciting and creative Millennium initiatives without addressing the most basic, down-to-earth issues of church life. There is little point in trumpeting a pioneering project when the welcome offered to newcomers is careless, cursory or even (it happens!) non-existent. **Symon Beesley** has produced a simple, user-friendly package that aims to help church leaders give their churches a timely and purposeful check-up.*

Briefing: A simple survey

People learn by involvement and discovery rather than by being told.

How Friendly to Strangers is your Church? is designed to help a church assess and improve the quality of its welcome to newcomers. Unlike many questionnaires, this one does not require a large sample of responses. Instead, it takes its inspiration from the commercial world's use of anonymous 'mystery shoppers'. The questionnaire is completed by two genuine, but 'planted', newcomers. Ideally these people should have little or no experience of church life.

Find a dark stranger!

You need to ask a leader from another church to find a couple of people who have never visited your church. Once two such people have agreed to act as 'mystery visitors', you can send them copies of the questionnaire. They will also need to know the 'time window' within which they should make their visit. Make sure they are warned not to 'blow their cover'; they shouldn't bring the questionnaire with them. Dark glasses, trench-coats and clip-boards should probably be avoided as well.

The questionnaire encourages the visitors to respond to aspects of the church that can easily be missed by its members whose perceptions may be dulled by habit. How does the church present itself to its community? Is it easy to locate? Once found, how accessible is it? Does it look attractive and cared for?

The responses may provide encouraging confirmation that things are going well; or they may provide some very thought-provoking home truths. As well as offering guidance on interpreting the information that the questionnaire produces, the booklet provides useful comparative information based on responses culled from churches in the Southampton Deanery.

It is possible to access the whole text of *How Friendly to Strangers is your Church?* via the CPAS website (see Resources file, page 63) or to purchase a copy from the author.

Pick'n'mix: Millennium Challenge

A national initiative to encourage people to go back to church on New Millennium Sunday (2 January 2000) includes ten practical goals to encourage churches to be welcoming, relevant and challenging. If you want your church to be this, sign up for the Challenge and work towards a newcomer-friendly service. It can easily be incorporated into your denominational style. There will be a resource book to accompany it, available from January 1999.

Pick'n'mix: Write a song

The aim of this initiative is to 'shake up our churches with your songs'. Anyone can have a go, from Graham Kendrick to someone who can put three chords together and create a tune. 'More than anything,' say the organizers, 'we want songs which challenge people to think about faith in everyday life and help churches to look at worship in a way which is dynamic, but holds on to the integrity of our gospel values.'

Pick'n'mix: Witness on cassette

An evangelistic, celebrity-presented resource tape to help you share your faith with friends, neighbours and colleagues – without blowing your relationship – is being produced jointly by *International Christian Communications* and *Fanfare for a New Generation*. Many Christians find it hard to ask their friends and colleagues where they are 'at' spiritually. This tape, entitled *Time to Make a Difference*, helps to pose the questions and give some answers through a series of short celebrity interviews in a relevant and non-threatening way.

You could use it as part of a strategy, culminating in a 'newcomer-friendly' service on the morning of the first Sunday of the new Millennium. A separate introductory teach-in tape and starter pack includes ideas on how to get the most out of the tape and how to prepare for the service (available January 1999).

Speciality: Home group Bible study

Look around with realism: Philippians 3:7-16

Key verse: Let us live up to what we have already attained (Philippians 3:16).

Icebreaker (10 minutes)
Brainstorm, with someone writing up your ideas on a large sheet of paper, what activities group members are involved in (a) in church, (b) in the community (including work) and (c) in leisure. Add in their skills and unique spiritual and practical gifts. What can you see from this about the group's corporate potential for service and witness?

Discuss (10 minutes)
Jesus summed up the attitude of many people to the present in the words 'Eat, drink and be merry' (Luke 12:19). To what extent is this true in your community? How is it expressed in concrete ways? Now be honest: to what extent does this attitude rub off on you and how does it affect your 'Christian' lifestyle?

Read and reflect (5 minutes)
Philippians 3:7-16
Note: This is one of Paul's letters from prison (probably Rome). Two words have strong images associated with them. 'Rubbish' (verse 8) means 'muck'; the King James Version translates it as 'dung'. It is not simply something no longer needed. 'Straining' and 'press on' (verses 13-14) capture the intensity of a runner or chariot driver nearing the finish of a race.

Analyze and apply (30 minutes)
1. What good things did Paul have which he counted as 'loss' and 'rubbish' (verses 4-8)? What parallels might there be for us? What good things do we sometimes have to lose because of another calling (e.g. an influential and well-paid person leaving a job to be ordained)?
2. Put into your own words what 'the surpassing greatness of knowing Jesus' means first for Paul and then for us. How might such an experience and attitude affect how we deal with (a) suffering or trouble, (b) the good times and good things of life? (Note what Paul says about good things in 1 Timothy 6:17-19.)
3. What is the difference between 'forgetting' what lies behind (verse 13) and *ignoring* the past?
4. Where has Paul, the successful apostle, got to at this late point in his life (verse 12)? Most of us reach a plateau of contentment where spiritual growth slows or stops altogether. How can we avoid this?

Quote to note and discuss (10 minutes)

'The "now" of boredom for many... may be interpreted as a past blocked by guilt, a future repressed by anxiety... so boredom becomes the emotional experience of the present. For the Christian, the release from past guilt is forgiveness, while future hope and therefore freedom from anxiety both make possible the enjoyment of the "now"' (James Houston, *I Believe in the Creator*). As we 'press on' how might we avoid the boredom which comes from unsatisfied daydreams or the frenetic embracing of whatever is 'new' for its own sake, and instead enjoy what God is doing now even though it is not complete?

Praise and prayer (10 minutes)

Thank God for where he has brought you so far. Praise him for all the good things you can enjoy. Hand over to him the things you are tempted to rely on. Pray that you and your fellow church members will learn to live for God now rather than reflecting ruefully on the past or dreaming of the future.

Pick'n'mix: The Open Book Project

The Open Book Project is a flexible scheme for local churches to encourage members of the public to reconsider the Bible and its message. Promoted by the Bible Society, it takes five key passages of Scripture with accompanying themes, which are:

- Creation, and Identity
- Exodus, and Freedom
- Exile and Restoration, and Justice
- Nativity, and Hope
- Cross and Resurrection, and Forgiveness.

There is a *Resource and Action Planning Pack* which lists over forty different ways of presenting these stories to people in our culture.

David Spriggs, the Project Director, writes that 'Our starting point is to engage people with the whole of God's story by telling carefully selected parts. Secondly, we can use many creative gifts with which to tell these stories, such as painting, sculpture, poetry, music, IT, web sites and so on. But people learn more by involvement and discovery than by being told. So it is important to involve people from the community in the events you choose to stage and then prayerfully leave God to work with them.'

WHAT? WHERE? WHO? AND HOW?

Find out more from our resources file!

PAGE 63

Bible community survey

This is produced by the Open Book Project. Finding out people's knowledge of and attitude to the Bible is a spur to action. You can add value to this by providing respondents with a 'thank-you gift' such as an invitation or free ticket to a related event or activity.

Special events

Among the ideas you could consider are:

- an attractively printed piece of Bible Story to give away
- a quiz night at the pub
- a Story-telling event at the local community centre

- a Cyber-net Café (with a free coffee and croissant for survey respondents!)
- enter the carnival with an Open Book theme float
- put on an exhibition of local historical interest – indicating the connections with the five themes of the Open Book
- challenge the humanist society to a debate about 'The kind of society we want' at the school bonfire bonanza, calling it perhaps 'The Big Bang'!

Inventory of interests and activities

Make a list of the professional, social and leisure interests of church members, so that they can be clustered together and released to do their own Open Book thing. Alternatively a church might like to look at its own activities and see how they can be given an Open Book spin. So, for instance, the Flower Festival could focus on hope, or the holiday club could organize events and teaching on the five issues, one for each day.

WHAT? WHERE? WHO? AND HOW?
Find out more from our resources file!
PAGE 63

FUTURE PERFECT?

➤ *LOOKING AHEAD WITH VISION AND COURAGE*

What kind of future does God want for his church? Too often we think the future means more of the present. But one thing is certain: things will change. Are we prepared to explore the possibilities of God's future, or do we settle only for preserving the present for as long as possible? This is the key question as the church approaches the Millennium. **Stephen Cottrell**, *the Bishop of Wakefield's Adviser for Mission, sets the agenda.*

Briefing: God's people on the move

The scriptures, sacraments and traditions of the church give us a compass but not a map. God has new things to show us.

The Bible describes the people of God as being on the move. 'For here we do not have an enduring city, but we are looking for the city that is to come' (Hebrews 13:14). It is this sense of being a pilgrim church that should shape our planning. In particular, there are four elements that make for valiant pilgrimage, and therefore for proper Christian planning.

We need to know where we are going

The big idea of the Christian faith is the kingdom of God. A vision of it should inspire, cajole, rebuke and determine all our planning: it is our compass, pointing beyond ourselves to God. Without this vision we will end up aping the kingdoms of the world.

The English word 'parish' comes from a Greek word meaning 'place of exile'. We should recover this sense of the life of the church as exile from our real home. This way we shall always keep moving.

We need to travel light

We must ask what it is that makes us distinctively Christian and what is secondary and weighs us down. We need to prune the church. The skilful gardener does not just cut back the dead wood – that is relatively easy – but prunes some of the living branches so that the whole plant flourishes. So we need to discern priorities for our life together and decide what is essential for the journey.

We need to work together

We are not lone explorers but an expeditionary force. The scriptures, sacraments and traditions of the church give us a compass but not a map. God has new things to show us. We need models of ministry and ways of being church that can be adapted by every culture, and which rejoice in a variety of expressions. They will utilize the gifts, contributions and insights of everyone.

Speciality: Home group Bible study

Our mandate to be the church for every person in the land will be expressed sociologically in the networks of individuals' lives as well as geographically in our neighbourhoods.

We will be companions in the faith. The word companion means literally 'one with whom we break bread'. The communion service gives us the model for our life together – a people blessed, broken and shared. We need to see afresh the mystery of Christ's presence with us when we break bread together. This will be our rations for the journey.

We need to share what we have received

We are followers in the Way of Christ. Everything we have received is given in order to be shared. We need to invite others to this way of life. Every human being knows that life is a journey, and every human heart shudders in the shadow of death. We can show that life is a pilgrimage, a journey home: our lives must be signposts to heaven. Then the future will be perfect.

Look forward with faith: Joshua 3:4

Key verse: You have never been this way before (Joshua 3:4).

Quote to note and icebreaker (10 minutes)
*'"I am looking for someone to share in an adventure that I am arranging, and it's very difficult to find anyone" [said Gandalf].
"I should think so – in these parts! We are plain quiet folk and I have no use for adventures. Nasty disturbing uncomfortable things! Make you late for dinner! I can't think what anybody sees in them," said our Mr Baggins, and stuck one thumb behind his braces, and blew out another even bigger smoke ring'* (J.R.R. Tolkien, *The Hobbit*). What 'adventures' have group members had? Were they planned or spontaneous? How did they feel at the time? What do others feel, as they hear of them? ('You wouldn't get me doing that!') Why do we both crave and fear 'adventure'?

Discuss (10 minutes)
Many people, especially in the church, are fearful of change. List down one side of a sheet of paper the reasons why this might be, and beside them list Bible verses or simple Christian ideas which might help them cope with this fear (e.g. fear of unknown/God knows it already).

Read and reflect (5 minutes)
Joshua 3
Note: The Israelites faced the river Jordan at the 'worst' time of year (verse 15). The normally shallow river was swollen by floodwaters and would have been well over 100 feet wide and ten feet deep. A landslide is often said to account for the temporary cessation of the flow. The ark of the covenant was the symbol of God's presence; while it was on the riverbed the people could trust that God would continue to hold back the water.

Analyze and apply (30 minutes)

1. Why did the Israelites have to consecrate themselves (make themselves ritually clean) seeing that God was going to perform the miracle anyway (verse 5)? What is the relationship between our purity and God's activity? Think of practical ways in which you and your church could 'consecrate' yourselves in readiness for God's work in the new Millennium.

2. The river was still flowing when the priests stepped in (verse 8). Faith often has to act before we have evidence that God will do what we believe he has promised. How do you think the priests felt at this point? How would you feel? What can you learn from this about 'stepping out in faith'? How might we know when the 'right' time is – how can we be sure we have heard God aright?

3. What did the Israelites know about the land they were entering (see Exodus 3:8; Numbers 13:27-29)? What do you know about the future plans God has for you and your church (compare with Mark 10:29-31)? Why do we always want to know more?

Discuss (10 minutes)

What is your group's vision for the future? Where do you want to be, what do you want to be doing, in five years time? Think about why you exist, and what God may require of you.

Praise and prayer (10 minutes)

Thank God that he has a good purpose for you. Ask him to keep you faithful so that you follow him step by step. Seek his strength to step forward not knowing what lies ahead, and to deal with the obstacles along the way.

Pick'n'mix: *Jesus* video

**WHAT?
WHERE?
WHO?
AND HOW?**
Find out more from
our resources file!
PAGE 63

First produced in 1979, the film *Jesus* is said to be the most authentic film in circulation on the life of Christ. Based entirely on Luke's narrative, it is available in 430 language versions and is estimated to have been seen by 1.3 billion people. Agapé, the distributors, are making an eighty-minute video version (the unedited film lasts for two hours) available for free distribution in church-sponsored video projects.

Church members visit neighbours to offer the video for loan (or as a gift), asking only of those who receive it the willingness to answer a short questionnaire a week later. If the viewers show interest when the questionnaire is collected, they are offered a free Millennium edition of the *Jesus* magazine which contains Luke's Gospel and stories of people whose lives have been changed by Christ. Two weeks later they will be invited to local discussion groups, but no pressure is put on them. All necessary materials are available from CPAS, and the *Jesus* video team have a telephone helpline.

FORGIVE THEM THEIR DEBTS

The Jubilee 2000 Coalition is campaigning to free a billion people in poor countries from the crippling burden of international debt. **Ann Pettifor**, *Director of the Jubilee 2000 Coalition, explains.*

Briefing: A worldwide campaign

Poor governments with high levels of debt divert precious resources from health, education, safe water and sanitation into debt servicing.

When the new Millennium arrives at least one billion people will not be celebrating. They live in countries with high levels of debt owed by their governments to Western governments and banks. So, while they can't celebrate, neither should we.

The vision for our campaign came from Leviticus 25. In this the Lord calls on the people of Israel to re-order their society periodically, to restore justice and balance to a community that had suffered economic and social degradation. Once every fifty years, they were to cancel debts, free slaves and restore land to its rightful owners. They were to sound the trumpet 'and declare liberty throughout the land'. The Hebrew word for trumpet is *jubel*, and it's this word that gives its name to our movement.

How international debt affects a billion people

There is no international bankruptcy law, so it is never possible to write off government debts, even when they have in effect become bankrupt, like Sierra Leone, Liberia, Rwanda or Burundi. This bankruptcy leads to economic and social degradation. Arrears build up, and then poor countries have to pay compound interest on the arrears. In the end they are paying interest on the interest.

Poor governments with high levels of debt divert precious resources from health, education, safe water and sanitation into debt servicing. Debt repayments are invariably sent to rich creditors, like the UK, Germany, the US and Japan, or to institutions dominated by the rich countries such as the IMF (International Monetary Fund), the World Bank, or the secretive Paris Club of creditors.

Comic Relief is very proud of the £26 million it raises every second year for poor people in Africa. Yet the poor nations of sub-Saharan Africa send back £24 million every day in debt repayments. For every £1 the West as a whole gives to developing countries, £3 comes straight back in debt repayments.

How debt kills people

Mozambique spends about thirty-three per cent of its budget paying off debts, and only eight per cent on education and three per cent on health. That is why debt kills. Each year more than 190,000 Mozambican children die before reaching the age of five and 10,000 Mozambican women die from childbirth-related complications, because their government can't afford basic health care. Its revenues are diverted into debt service.

Borrowers in the UK may not like making repayments, but at least they signed a contract. In Zaire, poor people were never asked to sign for any loans. After getting rid of their corrupt dictator, they've no choice but to pay back the debts he incurred.

No limits to liabilities

When Robert Maxwell fell off his yacht in the Mediterranean, the banks found his company was bankrupt. Both banks and pension funds demanded that Maxwell's sons accept some of the liability for the loss. But the British courts found in their favour that they enjoyed limited liability for their father's actions.

Not so the sons and daughters of Mobutu's Mozambique fiefdom. They now face unlimited liability for loans given in secret by powerful creditors, like the IMF and World Bank.

In the 1980s poor countries found that the value of exports like coffee, tea, cocoa, copper and sugar fell dramatically. But they can't pay off international debts in local currencies, only in dollars or sterling earned from international trade. So they got into difficulties, and the banks and IMF moved in.

As a condition for bailing out these countries, the IMF in effect repossessed their economies by imposing 'Structural Adjustment Programmes'. These require cuts in government spending, jobs and services, and removals of subsidies. Therefore local prices of bread and rice rise. Governments are also forced into privatizing national assets like airlines or telephone companies, which are nearly always bought by big Western companies.

World's biggest petition?

This 'repossession' of poor country economies by rich Western creditors leads to a new kind of slavery, which we say is profoundly unjust. We are calling for a one-off cancellation by the year 2000 of the unpayable backlog of debts of the poorest countries. We also want changes in the way loans are given to impose discipline, and transparency on lenders as well as borrowers.

We are collecting signatures for what we hope will be the biggest petition in history. We need your help in collecting signatures from friends, school, church, trade union, and local community. We are taking that petition to the leaders of the richest creditor countries (known as the G8). G8 leaders sit on the boards of the IMF and make key decisions affecting debtor countries. In 1999 they will be meeting in Berlin and in 2000 in Tokyo.

We are working together with a wide range of agencies including CAFOD, Christian Aid and Tear Fund. Our partners also include many black community groups with links in the South, many women's groups and the national and international trade union movement. We have supporters in sixty countries around the world.

**WHAT?
WHERE?
WHO?
AND HOW?**

**Find out more from
our resources file!**

P A G E   6 3

GENERATION 2000: YOUTH ON THE MOVE

➤ *THE SEARCH FOR MEANING*

How does the church – often overwhelmed and bewildered by Generation X – get through to this mass of people who feel alienated, disenfranchised and lacking in self-worth? **Steve Chalke**, *Director of Fanfare for a New Generation and International Director of Oasis Trust, describes the needs and offers some starting points.*

Briefing: The need to belong

'Never has a generation had so much opportunity and yet been so lost.' (Tony Blair, 1995 Labour Party Conference)

Generation X, the youth of today, is aspiring to a 'perfect world' full of opportunity yet desperately searching for meaning. Theirs is a communications world of the Internet, web sites, techno babble, pyscho babble and cyber space, a culture where advertisers and the media promote empty promises like 'Girl Power'. It is a generation looking for a better world, but not knowing how to find it.

Easy to be alone

We live in a largely dysfunctional society. You can shop from home, work from home, play video games alone at home. But home can be an empty shell. Today, more people than ever before are choosing to live on their own. As we come to the end of the twentieth century, we find a generation of young people living in an isolated and individualized culture.

Young people want to belong. They are looking to be a part of something, whether it's a community or a shared experience. When the Princess of Wales died, people of all ages, races and backgrounds flocked to London to join in the corporate grief. There was a sense of unity, of bonding, of sharing. That same feeling of belonging happens in football stadiums around the country.

Believing follows belonging

'When you believe, you will change and then you'll belong' is the traditional path trodden by many churches. But all research shows the model works best the other way round. Belonging, leading to belief, enables change. That was the way Jesus did it. His motley group of twelve developed into a team of disciples who were committed to him and to each other. The team developed as Jesus gave each one of them responsibility. It had its problems. But gradually the disciples grew into a cohesive group

Making The Most Of The

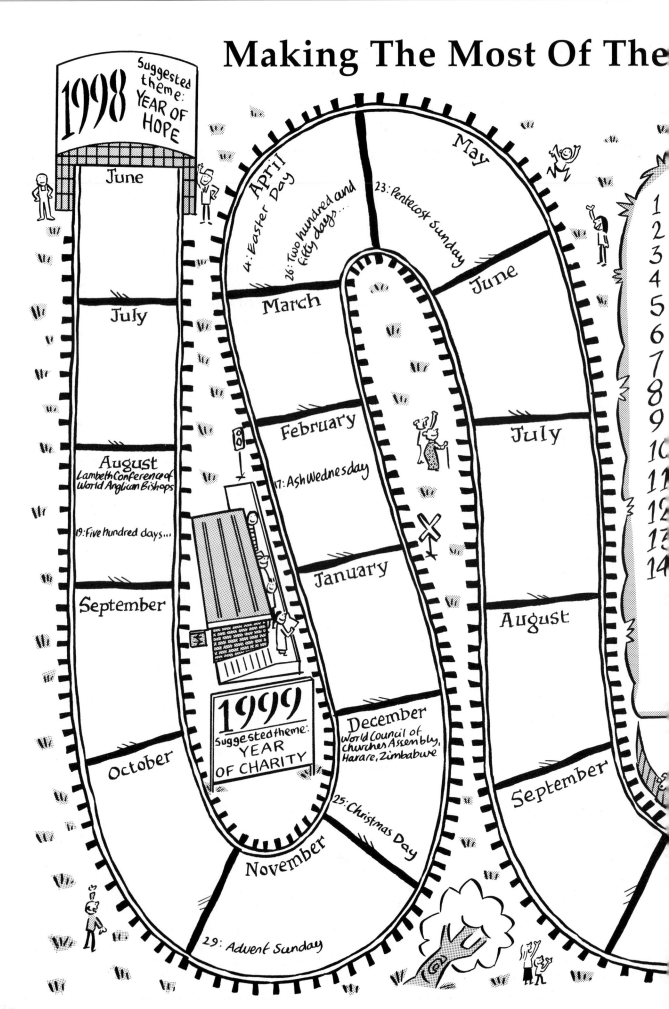

llennium – planning chart

December

15
16
17
18
19
20
21
22
23
24
25 Christmas Day
26
27 Bank Holiday

28
29
30
31 Millennium Eve!

January 2000

1
2
3 Bank Holiday

2000

January

February

March

8: Ash Wednesday

April

23: Easter Day

May

June

10: Global March for Jesus.
11: Pentecost Sunday

November

28: Advent Sunday

©CPAS

33

'I still haven't found what I'm looking for.' (U2)

who were entrusted and empowered.

So the church needs to develop models where young people feel they belong *before* they believe. We have to build relationships *before* we earn the right to share our beliefs and hopes. Your church may decide to put on a huge youth event to celebrate the Millennium. You may even bring in a specialist youth team to run an action-packed week of mission. But if this work among young people is going to be effective and lasting, there has to be time for developing relationships – both before and after events. Generation X craves relationship, not entertainment.

Time to talk

As relationships develop, there will be natural opportunities for discussing hopes, dreams and aspirations. There may be the discovery that life does have meaning after all – that it doesn't have to be a world of empty promises and lost opportunities. The young people may even see that hope lived out by the ordinary people around them who believe in God.

God didn't create us to live in isolation, to be alone. We were created to be with others. The church, more than any group, has to grasp the opportunity of showing young people what 'belonging' means. It's about welcoming them, including them, trusting them, giving them responsibility, empowering them. Generation 2000 need to know they matter.

GENERATION 2000 YOUTH EVENT

*It's essential that your young people are part of the planning team for an event like this, says **Sue Radford**, Project Director of Fanfare for a New Generation. As the event will be determined by your own particular group, this section will not offer you specific creative ideas. But it will give you some guidelines and a timetable for your planning.*

Briefing: Principles to follow

Be credible

Your event may well be competing with other Millennium parties and activities and has to have its own credibility. It's important to get some of your young people involved in the planning of the event – to let them shape and 'own' the ideas. Listen to their comments and feedback. You need to attract the friends of your youth group – as well as your own young people. Integrity is important. Parents will want to know their children will be in a safe environment – that there will be no drugs, no mixed sleeping arrangements – but that their children will have fun!

Be consistent

Start building relationships now! Young people will be suspicious if they are only ever invited to one event in the life of the church. Consistent role modelling is essential to build up trust with young people and parents.

Be creative
Think big! Don't set any limits in your brainstorming sessions. Don't be put off by practicalities straight away. Listen to the ideas from your young people.

Speciality: A year's countdown

12 months: start thinking
Get your young people thinking!

11 months: start planning
Get a planning team together and set up a planning meeting. Decide on the aim and target of your event:
- **Strategy** Is it a one-off, or will it be one of a series of events?
- **Date** Make sure it doesn't clash with another event
- **Venue** Book up as early as possible, checking facilities
- **Budget** Prepare a budget and fund-raising strategy
- **Book** any guests/artists (check fees!); decide on catering
- **Pray** Set up prayer networks to pray regularly for the event
- **Inform** church leaders and other youth groups in the area

6-10 months: get down to detail
- **Check** artists' PA requirements and book any PA, lighting equipment, etc. as necessary
- **Get the key idea** or theme in place six months before your date. Make sure you're getting enough support and helpers
- **Build relationships** in your youth group and make sure you have good links with parents. You may want to make your current youth work activity more open, so your own young people get into the habit of inviting their friends
- **Plan/book transport** if you need to help people to get there

3 months: check details
- **Check** that your guests/artists, caterers, etc. still have your date in their diary and confirm bookings in writing!
- **Check** the artists' PA requirements (or other resources) again
- **Prepare publicity** – invitations, leaflets, posters
- **Contact** your local newspaper/radio so they put your event into their Forward Planning diary
- **Plan** decoration of the venue (if appropriate)
- **Start** to plan any follow-up event

2 months: publicize
- **Prepare** press release
- **Distribute** posters
- **Sell** tickets (or send out invitations if you are not charging)
- **Encourage** your young people to start publicizing the event among their friends
- **Publicize** event in church/parish magazines
- **Make sure** there will be enough transport to get people home

1 month: get ready
- **Distribute** press release
- **Make check-calls** to guests, artists, venue, caterer, sound, lights, etc. to confirm date, timings, requirements
- **Contact** local media to see if they're interested in covering the event or interviewing young people
- **Get** as many resources ahead of the day as possible
- **Work out** programme for preparing venue
- **Work out** final programme and timing of the evening
- **Hold** production meeting; prayer/briefing meetings

On the day: go for it!
- **Check** on venue
- **Meet** artists and introduce them to hosts (if appropriate)
- **Get** refreshments for set-up crew and meal for artists
- **Hold** prayer meeting
- **Pay** artists

After the event: clear up!
- **Hold** de-briefing meeting
- **Arrange** follow-up meetings and events for your young people and their friends
- **Send** letters of thanks; pay all bills

SCHOOL BAG

*A major focus of Millennium activity will be on young people 'passing on the baton to a new generation'. A key focus for this will be in schools. **Sue Radford** describes the Generation to Generation project.*

Briefing: Generation to Generation

This practical and flexible project
- encourages and equips local churches to support and work alongside their local schools
- invests in the lives of young people in the community
- raises the profile of schools, Christians in education, schools workers, etc. among local churches
- allows participating churches to formulate their own ideas and to retain local ownership
- provides an opportunity to communicate a clear Christian witness to society as a whole.

By forging strong links with associated organizations, Generation to Generation offers resources, ongoing advice and support to churches that want to establish a longer-term strategy in their work with young people in local schools and communities.

Why schools?
Education and its related issues have become a major focus in today's society. Young people, teachers, parents and society as a whole are all keen to see standards raised and more resources

directed into schools. The church has an important role to play. By taking the initiative and working in partnership with schools and communities, the church can build up and resource young people, making a positive impact on their future and consequently on society as a whole.

How it will work

- Churches will approach local schools sensitively and appropriately to see how they can offer practical help.
- Working in conjunction with the school, the resulting project(s) can be flexible, tailored to suit each church and school, its resources and needs. These could include: equipping a school soccer team with new football kit; volunteers acting as nursery assistants, readers, etc.; funding a schools worker/counsellor; equipping a new computer centre; building a unit for excluded/difficult kids; youth projects; after school homework centres; getting involved at school board/governor level; helping with reading skills.
- All churches can do something, whether in isolation or working together. The project is neither church size- nor age-dependent. The projects are aimed at motivating the whole community.

How it will be implemented

A resource pack to get local churches started will be available from Easter 1999 as a step-by-step guide comprising everything you need to know including setting up contacts with the school; how to set up and run a Project Group; working out a strategy; how to communicate the vision; fund-raising suggestions; ideas for getting involved with schools; suggestions for projects; how to access useful resources, and how to work with other agencies and voluntary groups.

Pick'n'mix: JC 2000

This is the Millennium Drama Festival for Schools inspired by the life of Jesus. Claiming to be one of Britain's largest Millennium projects, JC 2000 aims to enable ten million young people to share in drama inspired by the life of Jesus, and for millions more to enjoy their creativity through television.

Every primary and secondary school in the United Kingdom will be invited to celebrate the Millennium by staging a theatrical performance inspired by the life of Jesus. All will receive assistance in preparing their productions which will be performed in over 2,000 local festivals and twelve regional festivals, culminating in a major UK-wide event, currently shortlisted to appear in the Greenwich Millennium Dome. JC 2000 is working in association with Independent Television and the festival will be reinforced through a series of programmes networked throughout the UK.

JC 2000 has the support of all churches and is being developed in close consultation with the leaders of other faiths to ensure that all pupils, parents and communities can share in this drama festival.

➤ *PUTTING CHRIST INTO LOCAL FESTIVITIES*

__David Hayden__, Vicar of Cromer, has been involved in community events for many years. Here he sets out the background and suggests how we can develop such involvement in local millennial activity.

Briefing: Make God's presence felt

I suppose my community involvement dates back to a park bench which needed to be dedicated. Or was it an extension to the bowls club house? Then came Honorary Chaplain to the Pier Theatre, and the Lifeboat and British Legion followed.

As a church we were invited to support the very sizeable carnival we have in Cromer. The vicar is invited to be one of the judges for the floats and one year I was asked to race a camel across the showground. Then there is judging shop window displays at Christmas, and joining the twinning association was rewarded recently with a journey to the south of France via Eurostar.

What's the point?

Someone asked me recently, 'Why do you bother? What is the point of it all?' I could say something really deep about incarnational theology but I might get it wrong! Instead, I will say how important it is that the church is seen to be part of the community and wanting to contribute to its life rather than being interested only in people who come to our church building. In Anglican churches the vicar is also given the task of being vicar to the whole community.

Being unofficial chaplain to the carnival led to an invitation to lead worship in the marquee as part of the carnival week. That was over ten years ago and it has now become a very popular and valued carnival activity. That is in addition to a carnival service in church for the committee and the new carnival queen.

Getting to know the town and district councillors has led to many invitations to meet people and lead special acts of worship. Taking part in the town's Christmas activities has given the opportunity to lead carol singing at the big event of switching on the Christmas lights and what follows in the pub afterwards. When HMS *Cromer* was given citizenship of the town we were approached to include an act of worship in the festivities.

However brief, these events cause many people who are not regular churchgoers to pause for thought and to recall that there is a God who cares for them.

Opportunities for all

The Millennium will offer churches a unique opportunity to provide specific Christian input to local plans for celebration. Is anything planned in your community? In many places, civic leaders would greatly welcome some good ideas. People desire to do something but are not sure what. In Cromer we have thought of building a harbour, which we cannot afford, and a signpost to the North Pole, which we can afford.

I know it has been very easy to get involved in my community and some places will be much harder. Nor do I want to add another 'ought' to clergy and church leaders who are already under stress. One good idea after another seems to come our way and some of us are weary in well doing and long to get back to the unbeatable combination of prayer and the Holy Spirit.

Encourage a new start

It could be a great encouragement for you, as it was for me, to visit the council member who is heading up the thinking of what to do in the community to mark the Millennium. (For us, it came under 'Leisure'.) It seemed obvious that the church ought to be involved from the outset. It was especially appreciated that we could use the Millennium theme of 'A Chance to Start Again'.

Perhaps the build-up to the Millennium will give us all 'A Chance to Start Again' in our contacts with the community of which we are part. The last years of this century have provoked tremendous discussion about the state of the nation and the world. The churches intend to sponsor a national debate about what we really want to see in the twenty-first century, which could give us another way in to local communities.

Pick'n'mix: Ideas for involvement

Produce the life of Christ

How about working with the community, including the schools, to have a major production on the life of Jesus which could be performed in three or four parts just before Pentecost 2000?

Candle power

The idea of the churches working together to give candles to all the homes in the community is popular in our area. These would be lit at 11.58 p.m. on 31 December 1999. (We have also talked about a special gift for the children of our town but we are wondering whether mugs would really be a good idea.)

Be peacemakers

Use the time up to the new Millennium to work with members of the community who are not church members, to do something to help others. What is really needed in your community? Are there long-standing problems between the church and community in your area? Could this be the opportunity to 'start again'?

Homes before domes?

Homelessness remains a major problem in many parts of our seemingly affluent society. It's possible that churches may want to focus on practical action against homelessness as part of a home-based peace and justice project for the Millennium.

As well as campaigning for homes for all, the housing charity Shelter offers practical help and guidance to people in crisis.

Open a shop
Why not rent an empty shop as a Millennium project? You can use it for simple outreach selling coffee and Traidcraft-type supplies, and a variety of second-hand items. You might make money (for the benefit of others, of course) and you might enable your churches to meet a whole range of new people.

Spread the idea
Give copies of the Churches Together in England booklet *A Chance to Start Again* to civic leaders.

Open the umbrella
Make use of the Churches Together 'umbrella' logo which all churches can use as part of their own publicity to remind people of whose anniversary it really is and to help them to see that they could use the Millennium to make a difference.

What not to do!
Have an open-air street party on 31 December 1999 with spray-can cream on the trifle.

Pick'n'mix: National events to join in

Beacon Millennium
Concept: Thousands of beacons, bonfires and fireworks displays will be lit right across the UK and the world at midnight on 31 December 1999. It will create an event in which everyone in the community can be involved. This has the potential of reaching people of all ages and groups and organizations such as Guides, Scouts, sports clubs, Lions, Round Table, youth groups, businesses (for sponsorship) and media interest.

Organization: Set up a working group and approach the local council to discuss building a beacon or large bonfire. Talk to local schools about the educational aspects of Beacon Millennium (history of the parish, Beacon designs, etc.). Discuss the possibility of a community event with local groups. Use it as part of a Millennium weekend strategy which will encourage people to go along to church on the morning of Sunday 2 January 2000.

Venue: This will depend on your local area, but ideally it should be in a central area, such as a village green or common, local hill, or town square.

The Great Walk
Concept: People of all ages throughout the UK will set off on The Great Walk (two miles) at noon on 31 December 2000 as a mass expression of national solidarity and to join in a friendly fundraising competition with their neighbours. Young, old, able-bodied, disabled, families, single people can take part.

Organization: Dream up imaginative ways of taking part in the walk and setting up friendly competition with your neighbours such as the fastest walk, the slowest walk, the youngest crawler, in fancy dress, walking backwards, tied to each other, joining hands, etc. Key contacts will include the Lions, Round Table, youth groups and organizations, Mums and toddler groups, schools, councillors, etc.

Millennium Run

Concept: Four lighted torches will set off from the four corners of the UK on 1 January 1999 on a national run. Runners will carry the torches through key cities and towns, where special services will be held to mark the 2000th anniversary of the birth of Christ. The Run culminates with the lighting of four main beacons in each of the principal capital cities at midnight on 31 December 1999. It will bring a Christian presence to civic festivities, encourage local participation, and raise funds for local charities. Churches will be able to take part in the special services along the proposed route.

Organization: Representatives from churches in the area will take along a special miner's lamp to the Millennium Run service. There will be an opportunity to light the lamp from the flame of the torch and keep it burning in your own church throughout the year as a symbol of Christ, the Light of the world. You can also use the flame from the lamp to light your local beacon on 31 December 1999.

2000 by 2000

This ecumenical project aims to encourage and fund a wide range of community projects around the country developed by social entrepreneurs in collaboration with churches and voluntary organizations. It aims to identify 2000 'moving spirits' who have a talent for bringing people together across social, economic and ethnic divides. More specifically, it would like to identify people who are already running, or could start, a Millennium project involving any age group which

- is relevant, deliverable and has broad community support
- builds bridges and works in partnership
- satisfies any unmet social need in areas such as the environment, the arts, drugs, crime and health
- will be completed by the end of the year 2000
- can range from the very simple (a neighbourhood 'makeover' campaign) to an extension of a larger piece of community regeneration work already underway.

**WHAT?
WHERE?
WHO?
AND HOW?**

Find out more from
our resources file!

PAGE 63

FOOD FOR THOUGHT

*Eating together is part of our social life, from Christmas parties to family funerals. The Millennium is a natural opportunity to organize community-based meals at which people on and beyond the fringe of the church will feel comfortable. **John Ledger**, Co-ordinator of the Archbishop of Canterbury's Food for Thought project, offers some suggestions.*

Speciality: Planning a Millennium meal

Prayer is so much more than just the support mechanism for evangelistic events. Prayer is the work of evangelism.

Aim
To extend friendship and build relationships with those in the local community or on the fringes of the church.

Plan
Talk and pray about the most appropriate meal-type event(s) for your area/village/town, which will be attractive to non-churchgoers as well as church members (see Pick'n'mix below). Ask if it should be aimed at one section of the community, or linked to some other local event such as a fireworks display or a civic service. Start planning early (1998) and let local authorities and other local groups know what you intend to do. Set up a small planning group.

Time
As the Millennium holiday weekend lasts four days (Friday 31 December 1999 – Monday 3 January 2000), avoid everything happening around Millennium midnight! Thus the Saturday, Sunday and Monday afternoons and evenings are possibilities.

Venue and catering
Go for a neutral venue where non-churchgoers feel relaxed and not intimidated by church premises, such as a hotel, restaurant, pub or village/community hall. You will need to make an inspired estimate of numbers if you are hiring a room at a catering establishment, and book it early. If it is the village/community hall, then it would be preferable to have outside caterers, otherwise recruit volunteers in the autumn, so that they can allow for it in planning their personal Millennium celebrations. (Bring and share is not the best arrangement when inviting outsiders.)

Who pays?
There are various approaches. Church members can invite and pay for their own guests. In some areas it is believed that those attending will value the event more if they make a contribution – maybe the full cost – but there can be special rates for families; the elderly, unemployed and low wage earners can be subsidized as necessary. Alternatively, church councils may support such events financially, as in a sense they are mini-missions to the community.

Entertainment

Before, during or after the meal there can be singing, sketches, games or other entertainment, even multi-media presentations if the facilities and expertise are available. Contributions should be sought from across the community, as well as from church members, and someone needs to co-ordinate this. It is an important witness in itself that Christians are seen to have fun together!

The Millennium slot

Think and pray how best to communicate the link between the year 2000 and Jesus Christ, and if appropriate to highlight the three New Start themes (see page 7). A talk by the church leader may not be the best approach! Can you use song, drama, dance or multi-media? People are more used to visual presentations than talks. At some events a brief acknowledgement of the significance of AD2000 by a local community leader from outside the church may also be appropriate. Much care and prayer needs to be focused on this part of the event; it should not 'jar' with the entertainment, but sit alongside it in an acceptable way.

Catch the vision

Communicating your plans to your church members and enthusing them to see the Christian opportunities around the year AD2000 is essential. However good the publicity, it will be their enthusiasm and willingness to invite friends, neighbours and relatives which will ensure that the event is successful and achieves its aim.

Publicity

Deliver information to every household in your area before Christmas 1999, and put up posters in shops, pubs, halls, etc. Indicate that people wishing to come need to contact the church office or other co-ordinator beforehand. Local authorities, papers and radio stations may have a Millennium events guide, so make sure yours are included. But getting a mention on the local radio's Sunday religious programme is not sufficient publicity to attract people from outside the church.

Keep in contact

Tell those attending that this is only one of several special events you are planning during the year 2000 and preferably give them details on a card. Avoid long and complicated verbal notices at the event! You may wish to consider following up with other meals during the year to strengthen relationships.

Prayer

Pray at every stage: when you start to plan; for the detailed planning and implementation; and especially for those to invite. Pray *briefly* at the end of an event for all present as they go forward into the new Millennium.

Pick'n'mix: A varied menu

Millennium lunch

A Millennium celebration lunch after the morning service on Sunday 2 January 2000 which includes a Millennium slot to illustrate by drama, song, word or dance whose birthday we are celebrating. Ideally this should happen in a neutral venue, following the guidelines above.

Millennium breakfast

Not a good idea to have this on 1 January, assuming that many people will have been up until past midnight! But for some churches it might be fitting to have a breakfast on the first day of the first week of the new Millennium (Sunday 2 January) to welcome it in and dedicate the future to God. This may be more of a fellowship event than an outreach event, of course, but you could be surprised at the people on the fringe who might like such a symbolic start. Churches which usually have an early communion service could add a breakfast to it on this occasion.

Millennium menu

If you plan a series of 'food events' or if you have contact with regular lunch clubs, you could do a countdown to the Millennium focusing on the foods which were common at a particular historical period. You could feature a different period for each meal, with a reflection on the lessons we can learn from the people of that time. Alternatively, you could base a series of meals on different cultures – Indian, Chinese, Israeli, French, etc. – reflecting what we can learn from each one. This could be especially appropriate in a multi-ethnic area.

Millennium picnic

Pentecost (June 2000) is the Church's birthday. A picnic with games and other fun events could be planned for that weekend, possibly ending with a celebration service.

➤ *COMMUNITY PRAYER CELLS*

What better – or simpler – way of marking the Millennium than making a serious commitment to pray for our neighbours? **Jane Holloway**, *Head of the Evangelical Alliance UK's Prayer Department, outlines the key elements of the 'Community Prayer Cell' approach to being 'good news neighbours'.*

Briefing: The idea

Community prayer cells are evangelistic groups which enable their members to pray, worship and witness in the communities in which they live, work or study. They meet in schools, workplaces and homes with the oversight of church leaders.

A prayer cell meets initially for twelve weeks with the clear understanding that members can leave if they decide it is not for them. Members are then usually asked to commit themselves to the group every six months.

Prayer is so much more than just a support mechanism for evangelistic 'events'. Prayer is the work of evangelism and missions. Prayer evangelism is biblical. In 1 Timothy 2:1-4, for example, Paul urges his readers to pray for everyone so that all will be saved and come to a knowledge of the truth.

Worldwide initiative

Three million people are reported to have come to Christ in eight years through this ministry in India.

Community prayer cells are being used by God in many places around the world. In Korea, prayer for non-Christian friends and neighbours plays an important part in church home cells. Churches are seeing dramatic growth as a result. In Argentina, Harvest Evangelism has pioneered new models of prayer evangelism using prayer cells. Mission 21 India reports that 1,600 Indian evangelists trained since 1985 have organized 100,000 'witnessing prayer cells' and that three million people have come to Christ in eight years through this ministry.

Types of community prayer cells

The community theme will be at the heart of much Millennium-based reflection. Community prayer cells encourage the widest possible definition of the word. The following are possible models:

- The **household** community prayer cell – made up of those who live under the same roof.
- The **area** community prayer cell – believers from different households who live in the same locality.
- The **workplace** community prayer cell – Christians working in the same business (or perhaps business park) or studying at the same college, but who do not necessarily live near each other.
- The **network** community prayer cell – a group of Christians who pray for a specific area or target group but who are not able to meet regularly. They keep in touch by phone, pray at specific times each week and meet when they can.
- The **home group** community prayer cell – forms part of the life of a regular home group/Bible study group if the members live in the same geographical area. Community prayer cells can be easily adapted for use in cell churches.

What a prayer cell member does

- Pray for 'neighbours' in your area, daily on your own and weekly in the group.
- Demonstrate God's love in practical ways and build bridges of friendship to the people you pray for.
- Contact neighbours to ask for their prayer requests.
- Be available to help them find answers to any questions they may have, drawing on the advice and resources of your church leaders as necessary.

- Be willing to explain how they could meet Jesus.
- Keep all prayer requests confidential.

Speciality: How to get a cell together

Pray before starting

Ask the Lord for guidance. Listen to him and watch for his leading. Consult church leaders (your own and others in the area) before starting any groups.

Pray for co-workers

These are people who could become prayer cell leaders, or who could form the nucleus of an initial prayer cell. Later, perhaps, it could split into several cells under their leadership. Ask questions such as 'Who would I like to pray with?' 'Where should the prayer cell be?' 'Do I live or work near Christians from other churches or my own church?' Share your concern prayerfully with one or two Christians. They should be prayerful people who have a concern for others. Also they should be people with whom you are comfortable.

Meet and share with them the vision of community prayer cells. You could use the book *Community Prayer Cells* at your first meeting. Make sure they understand the basic concept, the expected time commitment, and the potential value of this prayer ministry. Pray together. Take plenty of time before you make decisions.

Pray for group members

Working with your core-partners, make a list of other possible group members. Pray about who you could invite and decide who to ask first. Meet and share with them the vision of community prayer cells. Make sure they too understand the basic concept, the expected time commitment, and the potential value of this prayer ministry.

Ask them to make an initial three-month commitment. Assure them that they will be able to leave at the end of three months if it is not right for them. Explain that there will be an opportunity to make a subsequent re-commitment to the group every six months. Give them a week to pray for God's guidance. Invite them to get in touch if they have any questions. Meanwhile, pray for them and ask God to give them an enthusiasm for prayer evangelism in the area or workplace. Ask God to guide them, to remove ungrounded fears and to protect them from Satan's influence.

Meet up after a week so they can respond (either individually or together as a group). If they are hesitant, give them plenty of freedom to say 'no'. If they are unsure, give them more time. If they continue to be unsure, put them on hold and go on to other people on the list. Repeat the process until you have an initial group of three to five people.

WHAT? WHERE? WHO? AND HOW?
Find out more from our resources file!
PAGE 63

A WEEKEND TO REMEMBER

➤ *PLAN NOW FOR THE GREAT EVENT*

There will never be a weekend like it. This is the best chance we've had for 1,000 years to remind people of why our calendar starts with Jesus of Nazareth. We have had 2,000 years of faith, yet we live in a society that, by and large, turns its back on him. How can we use the weekend to remind people whose birthday it is? **Stephen Lynas**, *Archbishops' Officer for the Millennium and Churches Together in England Millennium Officer, explains how to take advantage of it.*

Briefing: A great opportunity

No one will ever have lived through a weekend like this one! Friday 31 December 1999 will be a New Year's Eve with a difference; Saturday 1 January 2000 will be the first day of the new Millennium; and then Sunday 2 January will be a day for Christians to gather at the beginning of a new era.

But before you get too excited, remember that it all comes straight after Christmas! So everything you do – whether as a church or in the wider community – will need very careful planning and forethought. The New Start themes (see page 7) will be useful, but remember this weekend is only a part of the whole Millennium process, which for many churches will start in September 1999 and run until the beginning of 2001. So don't put all your Millennium eggs in this weekend's basket!

Make a planner

You will find it helpful to put together a ten-day planning diary (see centre pages). Start on Christmas Eve (Friday 24 December), and finish on Monday 2 January – a Bank Holiday, thankfully! Mark in it all the events that are likely to affect your own congregation.

You'll need to allow for the fact that all sorts of people will be organizing Millennium weekend activities. Fortunately, not everyone will want to go to everything. And, especially on the Friday and Saturday, a lot of people will watch TV. There will be global coverage as each time-zone goes into 2000, and a lot of people will be up all night!

Three kinds of events

These will be:
- **family:** essentially private in the home when people can be with their nearest and dearest, with numbers from two to twenty-five

- **community:** these might be church events (like special services) or civic ones (like a firework party) with numbers from twenty-five to 1,000
- **large-scale:** which will vary from 10,000 people at a regional event, or ten million joining in an activity through TV, radio and the Internet.

The trick for your churches' events will be to arrange them in ways that allow most people the chance to choose to come.

Bigger than all of us

In all you do, remember that this is bigger than just your own church. This weekend will involve the whole population. As at a normal Christmas, people will be thinking about their families, being together, and celebration. Like a normal New Year, there will be some who are over-exuberant. There will also be those who, deep inside, are struggling to cope with their fear of the future.

Somewhere in this ragbag of events and emotions, your church has the chance to express the Christian gospel, which has something to say to everyone – happy or sad. So remember there will be a need to minister to the frightened and the lonely, as well as to the cheerful and the confident.

There will be global TV coverage as each time-zone goes into 2000, and a lot of people will be up all night!

Consider worship carefully

When it comes to worship please don't just redo what you do at Christmas! This is a one-off, and will need its own focus. So do you want to:

- **look back?** with thanksgiving at our Christian heritage; with regret at our failings; or
- **look forward?** confidently to facing the challenges of the new century; asking for faith and strength to cope with an uncertain future.

Perhaps you could set up a worship task force now to start putting together ideas for special services, using the Prayer and the Millennium resource packs.

Some dos and don'ts

DO make it clear whether this is an explicitly Christian gathering (with prayers, singing and maybe preaching) or an 'all-comers' event. Is it a service or a concert? A praise party or a festival? People like to know what they're in for.

DO consult widely with other local churches before you go firm on any plans. This weekend could be a great opportunity for Christians to do things together, and a cause for scandal if we work apart.

DO set someone the task of checking what other events are planned in your area. Talk to schools, and the local council. See if the Christian community can give some input to their events.

DON'T be ashamed to link up with national church initiatives. There's no need to go back to the drawing board, if someone else's design will work for you! So find out about things already planned for the weekend like Celebration 2000, Fanfare for a New Generation, Beacon Millennium, and the candles idea.

DON'T get defensive and embarrassed about providing some Christian content to the weekend.

Pick'n'mix: A weekend diary

> *A special service will help people to let go of the old and to welcome the new, to mark this special passing of time in a profoundly Christian way.*

Friday 31 December: put your hand in the hand of God

A special service, held in church in the early evening, to let go of the old and to welcome the new, to mark this special passing of time in a profoundly Christian way, before people go to join their friends at home or at public events. This is a day to say goodbye to the twentieth century, and to welcome the twenty-first. It provides a vehicle to give public acknowledgement to our deep-seated emotions about passing from one era to another, and to pray our way from one century to the next.

Combine powerful readings from Scripture about the passing of time, and the Jubilee message, with hymns and songs on the same theme. Allow plenty of space for prayer – both corporate and individual. Strike a note that is about letting go of the past, with all its baggage, and grasping the future, with all that God intends for us. Ask people to bring their Millennium candles to church and dedicate them before they go their separate ways to light them at midnight. Keep the sermon short and to the point! Let the Bible and the Spirit do the talking. Commission the congregation to be salt and light at the parties, and in the new Millennium.

Friday night (31 December): capturing the midnight moment

Involve the whole community in a shared act of silence and reflection just before the clock strikes midnight, by giving everyone a special Millennium candle and a copy of the Millennium Affirmation. This will capture the midnight moment in a way that is a clear gift from the Christian churches, but which encompasses the whole community, Christian and non-Christian alike.

Local churches will be able to distribute the special small candles in their holders, during Advent 1999. The holders carry the words: 'A gift from the churches of X town', and the text of the Millennium Affirmation. People are asked to take the candles with them wherever they go out on Millennium Eve, and to light them in a period of silence at two minutes to midnight. With thirty seconds to go, all say together the Millennium Affirmation.

This is for the whole community; it is not a 'Christian act of devotion' which only the very keen can take part in. It can take place wherever people gather: in private houses, at formal dinner-dances, out on the streets, on the village green.

Saturday 1 January: Celebration 2000

This is a nationally organized welcome to the new Millennium: five minutes of bells, followed by ten minutes of prayer. It is to give thanks for our safe delivery through 2,000 turbulent years,

and to pray for wisdom and strength for the future.

The Open Churches Trust and church bellringers will ensure that every church bell in the land is rung at noon, followed immediately by an imaginative act of worship for all, using a common pattern. Christians are encouraged to join together in their local cathedral, church or chapel for fifteen minutes at noon on 1 January 2000 to do three things:

- celebrate the birth of Christ
- give thanksgiving for the second Millennium
- seek a blessing on the third Millennium.

This initiative can involve every able-bodied bellringer (new recruits welcomed), and every Christian who should bring a friend to the service with them. It is a fitting way to end twenty-four hours of celebration around the globe, and a one-off event that can never be repeated.

It can take place in any church that has bells. But those without can still join in, by using a radio or TV relay, or by making their own joyful noise by using a band, or choir. Why not take a leaf out of the Old Testament and find someone who can blow a ram's horn (Psalm 81:3; Exodus 19:13)?

All weekend: open house

Invite the whole community to come inside the church building. It will be one way of offering spiritual space for those people who find they are troubled by the arrival of the new Millennium. Choose a day or two days, and let it be known that the doors will be open. Provide some very simple resources for enquirers (New Testaments, colourful leaflets about Jesus, and well-explained information about the church itself).

Above all, offer space for prayer and reflection: a candle standing for the Light of the World, an icon or a simple set of New Testament texts for meditation. Don't crowd people with too many stewards and coffee-stalls – let them find God in their troubles, rather than being troubled by well-meaning church members.

It needs to be organized by a small group of church members, dedicated to prayer and things of beauty, who care for those outside the regular congregation. Use a warm and welcoming part of the church, such as a side-chapel, or an altar area that breathes peace and strength through Christ. Free churches or churches with only one main worship area could provide a simple focal point in one part of the building.

Sunday 2 January: a special morning service

The first Sunday service of the third Christian Millennium could be used to commission church members to live as God's people in the twenty-first century, and to make a new start for themselves. By now, people may have had enough of 'special events' and want something low-key, amongst friends. The Methodist Church's traditional Covenant service provides one basis for a pledge between the people and God. Or you might want to produce something entirely local. If appropriate locally you could invite civic leaders, representatives of local institutions and employers.

Sunday 2 January: Celebrity concert

On Sunday 2 January 2000 Sir Cliff Richard, along with a host of well-known names, will take part in a musical Christian event. This multi-media event puts Jesus centre stage of Millennium celebrations and offers the opportunity for a moment of re-dedication and commitment to serving Christ. It is organized by Fanfare.

Speciality: Millennium exhibition

Gather ideas

In the early autumn of 1999, invite church members to contribute their own personal thoughts on two themes:
(a) the twentieth century – things I am glad to leave behind, and
(b) the twenty-first century – things I would like to see happen.

Under (a), some people will have deeply personal memories: relatives killed in a war, personal accidents or disasters, a career or way of life that has died out. Others will talk more generally about the Holocaust, Bosnia or the troubles of Northern Ireland.

It may be harder to get specific ideas under (b), although everyone, when pressed, will have some ideals about the future, whether it be personal goals or hopes for humanity.

It could be done as an opinion poll, or (perhaps with help from local schools), as a wider survey. If children are to be involved, artwork and banners could be prepared. The local library and museum may be able to help provide pictures and images of some of the things that people mention. Some people may be prepared to loan personal artefacts.

Assemble material

November 1999 (before the business of Christmas takes over) will be a key time to assemble the material. The Millennium Affirmation (which people will be using with their candles on Millennium Eve) could be used as a basic text to illustrate the storylines, and the Lord's Prayer would make a strong focus for the future.

The Christian framework for this is vital. You might choose to set it in a broadly biblical time-scale: from creation to the vision of the book of Revelation. Or you could build in an element that looks back over 2,000 years of local history, tying it in to the history of the Christian faith. You should choose some gospel soundbites to punctuate the whole – texts which speak of God's eternal love, of forgiveness for wrongs done, and hope for the future. For example: 'Jesus said: Go, and leave your life of sin' (John 8:11); 'I can do everything through him who gives me strength' (Philippians 4:13).

The whole congregation should be active participants. Special attention might be paid to the oldest and the youngest members!

WHAT? WHERE? WHO? AND HOW?
Find out more from our resources file!
PAGE 63

Choose a good venue

The exhibition might be in church or in school. It could be passed on to a library, shopping centre or civic centre foyer, or other public space. It is an opportunity to see our times through Christian eyes, and to share a vision with the whole community, and it can be as cheap or expensive as you wish.

Speciality: A service for the Millennium

Here is a service you can use as suggested or adapt to suit local needs. Hymns or songs may be inserted where you wish. It has been prepared by Jonathan Mortimer, curate of St Mary's, Crawley.

Service title

No present like the time.

Teaching point

All of our time is a gift of God to be used wisely, it does not belong to us. Therefore we should live in such a way that we are always ready for him to return.

Bible reading

Matthew 25:1-13 (the parable of the ten bridesmaids).

Before the service

Have this verse visible (on acetate, through a video projector, or in large letters): 'Keep watch, because you do not know the day or the hour' (Matthew 25:13). *Or*, the slogan: 'Why is it 2000?' Have a large gift-wrapped present on a stand at the front.

Opening to service

Service leader welcomes everyone to this service on the eve of a new Millennium.

If the resources are available (video projector, screen, black-out in church, someone to make video), introduce the service with this video. (Or you could make a tape/slide sequence.) Use the following scenes: a clock ticking and then the alarm goes off; count-down for a rocket launch; a clip of Neil Armstrong walking on moon and/or other significant moments in world history, the number 2000.

Service leader: Today we remember the passing of 2,000 years since God lived among us. Today is a momentous day. But in God's eyes, every day is. For each tick of the clock, each day, and each year is his gift to us. The number '2000' is as important to him as every year. God has given us all our time.

Opening liturgy

Service leader: He is the Lord and he reigns on high.
> *All:* **He is the Lord.**
> Spoke into the darkness, created the light.
> **He is the Lord.**
> Who is like unto him, never ending in days?
> **He is the Lord.**

And he comes in power when we call on his name.
He is the Lord.
Show your power, O Lord our God.

Song or liturgy

He is the Lord *(Kevin Prosch, Kingsway, 1991)* or liturgy:

This is the day the Lord has made.
We will rejoice and be glad in it.
This is the day the Lord has given.
We will rejoice and use it well.
This is the day when the Lord might come again.
We will rejoice and be ready for him.

Drama: God's time, our time

(You need a proficient keyboard player, or at least good tape-recordings of the music you want to use. During the readings from the Bible, the music to be played should be slow with a feel of 'majesty' about it; this is to contrast with the faster, staccato-like music to be played as a background to the sketches between. A form of 'Chopsticks' would be good for this. The purpose is to contrast the Creator of all time who is measured and in control of everything he does, and our own struggles with time and the stresses within it we create for ourselves.)

The music starts. If there are actors available who could strike a series of tableaux or poses during the reading, this could heighten the dramatic effect. If using them, there should be no more than three and their movements need to be well rehearsed so that they are synchronized. They start with backs to the audience, heads bowed.

Reader (best as an invisible voice speaking into a microphone): In the beginning God created the heavens and the earth. Now the earth was formless, and empty, and darkness was over the surface of the deep.
And God said, 'Let there be light' *(Actors turn round, heads lifted up)*, and there was light. *(Actors raise up arms towards sky and slowly bring them down during the next lines)* God saw that the light was good, and he separated the light from the darkness. God called the light 'day', and the darkness he called 'night'. And there was evening, and there was morning – the first day.

The music changes to *Chopsticks*. Actors in pose turn round with backs to the congregation. The music starts loud enough to set the tone of the next action, but then goes softer to form a background.

Parent (comes on stage putting on coat): Come on you two! We're late! We should be at school now, they'll be taking the register any minute. Now, where's the car key? *(To imaginary child upstairs)* Well, go and get it then. I'm sure I put it in my pocket! Sorry? Oh no! Why didn't you go before? You've been playing with the guinea pigs the last half hour – you could have gone then... ah, here is the key, knew I'd got it somewhere. OK, we're off. *(Leaves stage from the opposite side from which they came on)*

The music changes back to opening melody.

Reader (as above): Then the Lord answered Job out of the storm. *(Actors turn round)* He said: Where were you when I laid the earth's foundation? *(They point questioningly towards the congregation)* Tell me, if you understand. What is the way to the abode of light? *(They point upwards)* And where does darkness reside? Can you take them to their places? Do you know the paths to their dwellings? Surely you know, for you were already born! *(Ironic gesture towards congregation)* You have lived so many years!

The music changes back, actors turn round with backs to the congregation again.

Enter boss with secretary.
Secretary: And then at 9.15 you have the meeting with Rogers from Sales. At 9.30 the car is there to take you to the airport. On the way you'll get calls from Manchester, L.A. and Cape Town about the proposed take-over.
Boss: What time's the meeting at the other end?
Secretary: It's at 11.30, so there'll be just enough time to speak with Bridges... *(They exit from opposite side)*

Music changes back.

Reader (as above): Who of you by worrying can add a single hour to his life? *(Actors turn round)* So do not worry saying, 'What shall we eat?' *(They eat)* or 'What shall we drink?' *(They drink)* or 'What shall we wear?' *(They point to their clothes)* For the pagans run after all these things, and your heavenly Father knows that you need them. But seek first his kingdom and his righteousness *(They kneel and pray)*, and all these things will be given to you as well. Therefore, do not worry about tomorrow, for tomorrow will worry about itself. Each day has enough trouble of its own.

Music changes back.

Man enters speaking into mobile phone: I'm sorry, Mother, it's just not very convenient. Well, if you'd been able to give us more notice it would have been fine. But this weekend we're just totally tied up: Ben has got football all Saturday, Susi's revising for exams, and I promised Jean we'd be going to get the furniture from Croydon. We just don't have time... *(Exit)*

Music changes back. One of the actors who has been miming turns round to speak these last words. The two on either side of him kneel facing him.

Actor: Jesus says, 'Behold, I am coming soon! My reward is with me, and I will give to everyone according to what he has done. I am the Alpha and the Omega, the First and the Last, the Beginning and the End.'

Prayer of Confession

This can come straight after the presentation above, accompanied by the music above to make the connection clear.

Service leader: We remember before God how we have misused the time he has given to us.

God our Father, you who created heaven and earth; you who made night to follow day; you who made us to enjoy everything you had made, we are sorry that we forget you. Dear Father, forgive us.

All: **Save us and help us.**

Service leader: You are faithful and do not give up on us. But we get impatient when others do not fit in with our own plans. Dear Father, forgive us.

All: **Save us and help us.**

Service leader: You supply us with everything we need day by day. But we worry that you might forget us. Dear Father, forgive us.

All: **Save us and help us.**

Service leader: We are so busy organizing our own lives. We have no time to listen to you. Dear Father, forgive us.

All: **Save us and help us.**

Absolution

Almighty God, who in Jesus Christ has given us
a kingdom that cannot be destroyed,
forgive us our sins,
open our eyes to God's truth,
strengthen us to do God's will
and give us the joy of his kingdom,
through Jesus Christ our Lord. Amen.

(From Patterns for Worship, p.51 Church House Publishing, 1995)

Reading

To illustrate the reading:

1. Story Find someone who can tell a real-life story of something they forgot to do, which then had disastrous consequences. For example, forgetting to change oil in the car (fits the reading well!), not checking the batteries in the smoke alarm at home which then doesn't work, not feeding the guinea pigs. Alternatively, ask someone to describe how they look after something very precious to them, such as a valuable musical instrument, a pet, their car.

Teaching point: We always have time for things that are important enough to us. The foolish bridesmaids were foolish because they simply forgot the importance of their job. Their lack of oil was a sign of their wrong priorities. How important is it to you that Jesus has given you a job to do? Have you forgotten him?

2. Visual aid. A diary, a calendar, a Psion organizer, a clock, watch, alarm radio, etc.

Teaching point: We can measure our time, but we can't control it. Time is from God and is to be used for his purposes. If you were had up in court for being a Christian, would there be any evidence in the way you spend your time to convict you?

3. Visual aid. A birthday party invitation. Imagine the best party you could ever go to. (Get ideas from the congregation of what this could be like.) There are hundreds of friends, lots of food, everyone is laughing, music is playing in all the rooms. What's missing? Nothing. But one person is. Imagine a party, and no one has thought about the person whose birthday it is.

Teaching point: That was how the foolish bridesmaids treated the bridegroom. It was meant to be the wedding banquet in honour of him and his bride. But they had let him down, they just weren't ready for him to turn up. It's how Jesus is treated at his birthday, every year, including this the 2,000th anniversary of his birth. What is the difference between a wise and foolish bridesmaid on this day? The wise ones would be ready for Jesus to turn up, they'd always be ready to welcome him.

Unpacking the present
Inside the large present are a briefcase, a school exercise book, a duster, a lunch-box (with a picture on it of the latest Disney film). What are you most likely to be carrying this coming year? Wherever you go you will have the chance to do something or be something that says, 'I want to show that I know Jesus and I am ready for him to return.'

Challenge: 'Whatever you do, work at it with all your heart, as working for the Lord, not for men, since you know that you will receive an inheritance from the Lord as a reward' (Colossians 3:23-24).

Act of commitment
Spend a minute of silence reflecting on the momentous passing of time. Then use the following prayer together:
Dear God our Father, thank you for sending your Son for my sake 2,000 years ago. Thank you that he died to bring me to you. I turn to you again. I commit the days of my life to you. Please use me to do your will. I want to be ready for your return. Amen.

Song
'I want to serve the purpose of God' *(Mark Altrogge, © People of Destiny/ Thankyou Music, 1982)*

At the end of the service
As the congregation leave, give each a sticker or badge with the question: 'Why is it 2000?'

PENTECOST 2000

➤ *BIRTHDAY CELEBRATIONS*

*With the noisy exuberance of the 'new year' events behind us, Pentecost 2000 could offer the ideal opportunity for the Church to celebrate its birthday in a variety of creative, exciting and attractive acts of worship and witness. **Jan Goodenough**, a writer from Cambridge, offers some ideas.*

Briefing: Celebrating Pentecost

The Holy Spirit came upon a group of less-than-confident disciples and transformed them. After the dynamic events of Pentecost, they proclaimed Jesus fearlessly through their words and actions. A community of radically changed human beings began on that day in Jerusalem. The same Holy Spirit has never ceased performing the same extraordinary work as he fills and changes ordinary men, women and children so that Jesus may continue to be 'incarnated' in the world through his body, the Church.

Pentecost points us to the amazing origin of our faith. It challenges us with the awesome responsibility with which we are entrusted – and it comforts and encourages us by reminding us that we need never rely on our own puny resources for the power that's needed to fulfil that responsibility. It's a birthday celebration which should inspire and motivate those already in the Church; it also provides an ideal opportunity to invite people of other faiths and none to join us in our festivities.

The Pentecost weekend of 10-11 June 2000 may witness the culmination of the churches' Millennium celebrations. The fact that the weekend will be unencumbered by secular activities may make it possible to plan events that we can invite people to without the worry of 'butting in' to their own Millennium parties. And it has the advantage of happening at a time of year when, theoretically at least, outdoor activities are likely to be attractive.

Pick'n'mix: Parties and festivals

Church birthday party

Plan a birthday party for the church and invite the whole community: no fund-raising, no hidden agenda, no strings. Make it as much of a community event as possible. (Cast your mind back to the street parties of the 1977 Silver Jubilee celebrations.) Design and make a birthday-card invitation which could be distributed throughout the neighbourhood.

Festival of creativity

Why let Edinburgh, Aldeburgh and Notting Hill have all the fun? Pool the creative abilities represented in your church to celebrate

Pentecost in a festival focusing on music, craft, art, poetry, dance and drama. Transform your buildings into a community arts centre and invite the whole neighbourhood for an extravaganza of entertainment, performance and celebration that points to God the Father of all creativity.

Speciality: An all-age service for Pentecost

Title: Power for all

The preparation

Leader: Jesus said: You will receive power when the Holy Spirit comes upon you; and then you will be my witnesses (Acts 1:8).

All: **Lord, help us to love you that we may obey your command. Give us the Spirit of Truth. The world cannot accept him because it does not recognize him. Help us to recognize him; help him to live in us, in Jesus' name. Amen.**

Leader: Peter said: I now realise how true it is that God does not show favouritism, but accepts people from every nation who fear him and do what is right (Acts 10:34-35).

All: **This is the message God sent to the people of Israel, telling the good news of peace through Jesus Christ, who is Lord of all** (verses 36-37).

Leader: When the day of Pentecost came, they were all together in one place. Suddenly a sound like the blowing of a violent wind came from heaven and filled the whole house where they were sitting. They saw what seemed to be tongues of fire that separated and came to rest on each of them. All of them were filled with the Holy Spirit and began to speak in other tongues as the Spirit enabled them (Acts 2:1-4).

Hymn O Holy Spirit breathe on me (*Mission Praise* 500)

The ministry of the word

Reading Acts 5:12-16
Hymn The King is among us (*Mission Praise* 650)
Reading John 10:22-42
Talk Power for all
Hymn I hear the sound of rustling in the leaves of the trees (*Mission Praise* 274)

The creed

Leader: Let us declare our faith in the one, true and living God, the Father, the Son and the Holy Spirit.

Prayers of penitence

Leader: Jesus says: Repent, for the kingdom of heaven is close at hand.
Let us turn to him and let his light cast all that is behind into the shadow, confessing our sins in penitence and faith.

All: **Lord of all power, all knowledge, to whom no place is strange,**
We lay our lives before you in humility, by your grace.
Like children we have disobeyed,
Without heed, without trust,
We have wronged you and each other,
In our minds, in our hearts,
In our words, in our actions,
Through ignorance and lack of strength,
Through wrongful acts and headstrong will.
We are sorry. We put this behind us.
We ask that we may be made worthy in your sight
By the power of your Son's redeeming sacrifice.
Grant us the power of your Holy Spirit,
In life renewed and rededicated to your service,
To the glory of your name. Amen.

Leader: God is love. Trust that he forgives all who turn away from wrong. Trust his mercy. May he raise up the fallen, heal the hurt and strengthen all of us in faith, hope and love that we may at last praise him eternally. Through Jesus Christ our Lord. Amen.

Hymn When I feel the touch *(Mission Praise 753)*

The intercession
The Lord's Prayer

The Church and the World

For those in power to strive to lead as Christ showed by his example, enabling those in his care to fulfil the talents given to them by God. May the church demonstrate by example.

The Church

For those in church authority in each locality to be renewed by the Holy Spirit, to show the energy of the disciples at Pentecost and to have faith for a new vision and a new understanding of Christ in the new Millennium.

Royalty and State

For those in secular authority that by their example our nation might shine as a beacon to other countries in the ways of justice, peace and obedience to God's will. May we also be as open to learn by example as to set it.

Our communities

For families, friends and neighbours: help us to honour one another, giving greater priority to others than to ourselves. May we recognize strengths and abilities in others more clearly, be more willing to encourage them and actively seek to encourage them.

The Suffering

For the Holy Spirit to be set free to heal those who suffer in any way.

The Dead

Remembering those who have died, we thank you for their lives. We thank you for the part they played in furthering your plan, even if this may not be plain to us now. We thank you for their place on earth in history and ask that you comfort us through our memories of them. Grant that we, too, may share eternity in your kingdom.

Rejoicing in the fellowship of..., we commend ourselves and all Christians to your perfect love. Merciful Father,

All: **accept these prayers**
for the sake of your Son,
our Saviour Jesus Christ. Amen.

Hymn   Spirit of the living God, fall afresh on me (*Mission Praise* 613)

Acclamation

Leader: Since the dawn of time, Lord God, you have kept faith with your people:
All: **Your word created time and space.**
Leader: A day is as a thousand years to you,
All: **A thousand years is as a breath.**
Leader: You have determined all things from the beginning,
All: **In you there is no end.**
Leader: Living and eternal God,
All: **Lord of all nations,**
Leader: Blessed be your name,
All: **Blessed be God for ever.**

The Dismissal

Leader: May the Spirit of Truth light the new Millennium as he has lit the last. Enable us to see that light more clearly. Grant that we may go out in the power of the Holy Spirit, with grace, energy and love to fulfil your purposes, that we may impart a new vision of Christ to the world.

A Blessing

Leader: So we say to each other:
Left: **Deep peace of the running wave to you;**
Right: **Deep peace of the flowing air to you;**
Left: **Deep peace of the quiet earth to you;**
Right: **Deep peace of the shining stars to you;**
Left: **Deep peace of the gentle night to you;**
Right: **Moon and stars pour their healing light on you;**
All: **Deep peace of Christ the light of the world on you;**
All: **Deep peace of Christ.**

(Ancient Celtic blessing)

Hymn   Breathe on me, Breath of God (*Mission Praise* 67)

Leader: Go in peace to love and serve the Lord.
All : **In the name of Christ. Amen.**

Talk

Notes: If possible, slides of a volcano, forest fires raging out of control, a house on fire, a cosy fire in a grate and a candle would suggest a range of associations.

Talk about a volcano. It is unstable, unpredictable, destructive and beyond control. Forest fires can leap from tree to tree and kill everything in their path. A house fire can grow in minutes from a dropped cigarette or a small electrical fault into a force that tears through a building destroying whatever is there. But a controlled fire is magnetic, hypnotizing, warming, soothing. It draws people. A candle's single flame has been used for centuries as an aid to meditation. It focuses attention and symbolizes a variety of Christian themes: constancy, light in darkness, faithfulness, hope.

It could be argued that the flames over the disciples' heads at Pentecost illustrate the perfection of controlled fire, but there is another way of interpreting the symbol. Imagine that the fire of the Holy Spirit is to fire as anti-matter is to matter:

(Overhead)

- it is not destructive: it is creative
- it did not burn: it healed
- it is not dominating: it is enabling
- it does not need to be controlled: it needs to be set free
- fire rages: the fire of the Holy Spirit radiates the energy of joy and peace.

The only attribute that the fire of the Holy Spirit has in common with material fire is its potentially unstoppable energy.

For the last 2,000 years people have organized society in terms of power structures: top down, hierarchy, authority; bottom up, conformity or rebellion. Think of any institution and you can see a power culture in operation: work, schools, government, hospitals, churches. There are ways of doing things which take a while for the uninitiated to find out – explicit and implicit rules. People either conform or rebel and tensions result.

Jesus gives us an alternative vision:

(Overhead)

- he enabled the weakest: he built his church on a man who betrayed him through cowardice, who chose to deny knowledge of Jesus in an effort to save his own skin

- he raised up the downtrodden: the woman who poured ointment over his feet was scorned by the virtuous disciples who bemoaned the waste of material wealth in spilling costly perfume over Jesus' feet, but lifted up by Jesus, who valued her intention

- he healed the sick: lepers who were outcast were included by Jesus, healed and restored

- he loved the unlovable: tax collectors, prostitutes, lowly people of no wealth or standing

- he included when others sought to exclude: Gentiles as well as Jews, Samaritans and sinners, Romans and Greeks

- he gave all his power away: the Almighty born as a baby into a time of danger, totally dependent on his parents; he used his power for the benefit of others to his own personal cost; he gave his life so that the people of this world could be saved; through his sacrifice he enabled God's power to be released through the Holy Spirit so that we, too, can share in it.

At the start of a new Millennium, Jesus is still waiting for us to grasp this basic Christian truth fully and to put it into practice in our lives. If we can put behind us the struggle for personal power, the exclusiveness, the jealousies, the prejudices, the pride, the snobberies involved in worldly power cultures, then we will start the new Millennium with a vision that will change whoever we come into contact with.

Who are you sitting next to right now? Do you know that person well enough to know what gift God has given them to make them special? Spend a few minutes now, overcome your embarrassment, and just talk to each other bearing this idea of enablement in mind. Oak trees grow from acorns.

Pause

Enablement means that instead of putting others in their place, you enable them to fulfil God's purpose for them. To do this we must become sensitive to the gifts of others. We must seek to know and love them rather than slotting them into our days grudgingly. It means honouring other people. It means discerning their talents. It means encouraging them to develop latent skills. It means delegating power so that others can increase in responsibility. It might mean relinquishing your own role to enable someone else to develop and finding a new role for yourself. It means following in the shadow of Christ when he allowed himself to be debased to the point of being killed as the lowest of the low so that he could raise us up on the last day.

If enough people understand and take this on board, we will change the culture we live in as salt enhances a plate of food or a small candle illuminates a dark place. Perhaps both the hardest and the easiest, certainly the most essential, place to start would be with those closest to us, in our family and in our church. You could carry on chatting with the person you spoke to earlier after this service.

RESOURCES

WHAT?
WHERE?
WHO?
AND HOW?

This is it! Numbers refer to the pages.

■ Books, Videos and Other Resources

8   A Chance to Start Again
The booklet can be obtained in packs of 25, price £6.25, from Church House Bookshop, 31 Great Smith Street, LONDON W1P 3BN *(Tel: 0171 340 0276/7; Fax: 0171 340 0278).*

12   Millennium Worship Packs
If you want to know more, write to Janice Price, Board of Mission, Church House, Great Smith Street, LONDON SW1P 3NZ *(Tel: 0171 222 9011).*

21   Church visitor-friendly audit
You can download this from the CPAS website (http://www.cpas.org.uk) or obtain a copy of *How Friendly to Strangers is your Church?* by writing to The Rev Symon Beesley, 8 Shales Road, SOUTHAMPTON SO18 6NR. Please enclose £2.00 to cover the cost of photocopying and compilation.

22   Time to Make a Difference (cassette tape)
Details from Fanfare in partnership with ICC. Contact ICC, Silverdale Road, EASTBOURNE BN20 7AB *(Tel: 01323 643341).*

24   Open Book Project
The Churches' Resource and Action Planning Pack is available from Bible Society, PO Box 1100, SWINDON, Wiltshire, SN5 7DG *(Tel: 01793 418100).*

28   Jesus video
All the essential materials needed to help you run your own Millennium Jesus Video Project are available from CPAS, including Millennium *Jesus* videos, magazines, free offer leaflets, record sheets and briefing materials. For further advice, contact: The Jesus Video Project: Agapé, Fairgate House, Kings Road, Tyseley, BIRMINGHAM B11 2AA *(Tel: 0121 765 4404; Fax: 0121 765 4065; email: jvp@agape.org.uk).*

44   Community Prayer Cells
Full details and a training course for starting and running these can be found in *Community Prayer Cells* by Jane Holloway, published by CPAS, price £7.50. It may be ordered direct from CPAS Sales Orderline *(Tel: 01926 335855).*

Further reading
Michael Rees, *Celebrating the Millennium in the Local Church*, Grove Books, £2.25.

■ Millennium Projects and Organizations

9   Anno Domini (Evangelical Alliance)
Contact Brian Clews, Anno Domini, PO Box 680, MAIDENHEAD SL6 9ST *(Tel: 07071 202000).*

10   Y2000? (badge)
For details contact Y2000, 10 Marston Avenue, CHESSINGTON, Surrey, KT9 2YJ *(Tel: 0181 287 3147; email: info@7-2000.com).*

22   New Millennium Challenge to the Churches
For more details contact Sue Radford at Fanfare, 115 Southwark Bridge Road, LONDON SE1 0AX *(Tel: 0171 450 9070/1).*

22   Songs for the New Millennium
For more information contact Anne Richards, Songs for the New Millennium, 37 Hymers Avenue, HULL HU3 1LL *(Tel: 01482 444832).*

29   Jubilee 2000 (releasing debt)
If you want to join the campaign or receive more information contact Jubilee 2000 Coalition, PO Box 100, LONDON SE1 7RT *(Tel: 0171 401 9999; Fax: 0171 401 3999; website: http://www.oneworld.org/jubilee2000).*

36   Generation to Generation (schools project)
Details from **Fanfare for a New Generation**, 115 Southwark Bridge Road, LONDON SE1 0AX *(Tel: 0171 450 9070/1).*

37   JC 2000 (Millennium Drama Festival for Schools)
For more information contact David Senior, JC 2000, 36 Causton Street, LONDON SW1P 4AU *(Tel: 01625 590149).*

39   Homes before domes?
For more information contact Fiona Head, Churches and Communities Section, Shelter, 88 Old Street, LONDON EC1V 9HU *(Tel: 0171 505 2000).*

40   Beacon Millennium, Great Walk, Millennium Run
For details write to: Bruno Peek, Beacon Millennium, 21 Coverdale, Carlton Colville, LOWESTOFT, NR33 8TD *(Fax: 01502 580671)*.

41   2000 by 2000
For more information please contact the Project Director Libby Brayshaw, 2000 by 2000, PO Box 14785, Bromley by Bow, LONDON E3 3SJ *(Tel: 0181 983 3816)*.

49   Bells – Celebration 2000
Find out more from: Celebration 2000 *(Tel: 0171 240 0880; Fax: 0171 240 1204)*.

50   Open Churches Trust (ecumenical worship) – Celebration 2000
Ecumenical act of worship for 1 January 2000 details from The Open Churches Trust, c/o The Really Useful Group Ltd, 22 Tower Street, LONDON WC2H 9NS *(Tel: 0171 240 0880; Fax: 0171 240 1204)*.

Official Bodies

Department for Culture, Media and Sport
Contact: Warwick Hawkins *(Tel: 0171 211 6182)*

Millennium Commission
Contact: Ian Brack, Policy Manager *(Tel: 0171 880 2020)*

The New Millennium Experience Company
110 Buckingham Palace Road, LONDON SW1W 9SB
Contact: Kathleen Bowie *(Tel: 0171 808 8350)*

UK Church Bodies

Council of Churches for Britain and Ireland (CCBI)
Inter-Church House, 35-41 Lower Marsh, LONDON SE1 7RL
Contact: The Rev Donald Elliott *(Tel: 0171 620 4444)*

Churches Together in England (CTE)
35 Lower Marsh, LONDON SE1 7RL
Contact: The Rev Bill Snelson *(Tel: 0171 620 4444)*
Millennium Office: Church House, Great Smith Street, LONDON SW1P 3NZ *(Tel: 0171 340 0250)*

Churches Together in Wales
11 St Helen's Road, SWANSEA SA1 4AL
Contact: John Winton *(Tel: 01222 708234)*

Irish Council of Churches
Inter Church Centre, 48 Elmwood Avenue, BELFAST BT9 6AZ
Contact: Dr David Stevens *(Tel: 01232 663145)*

Other Church Bodies

Church of England
Millennium Office, Church House, Great Smith Street, LONDON SW1P 3NZ
Contact: The Rev Stephen Lynas *(Tel: 0171 222 9011 or 0171 340 0250)*

Roman Catholic Church
Contact: Mgr Nicholas Rothon *(Tel: 0171 821 5411)*

Evangelical Alliance
Whitefield House, 186 Kennington Park Road, LONDON SE11 4BT
Contact: Brian Clews *(Tel: 0171 207 2100)*

Inter Faith Contacts

The Inter Faith Network, 5-7 Tavistock Place, LONDON WC1H 9SN
Contact: Dr Harriet Crabtree *(Tel: 0171 388 0008)*

The Council of Christians and Jews
Drayton House, 30 Gordon Street, LONDON WC1H 0AN *(Tel: 0171 388 3322)*

The World Congress of Faiths
2 Market Street, OXFORD OX1 3EF *(Tel: 01865 202751)*